# TRUE TO LIFE

INTERMEDIATE

*Ruth Gairns*
*Stuart Redman*
with *Joanne Collie*

PERSONAL STUDY
WORKBOOK

**CAMBRIDGE**
UNIVERSITY PRESS

PUBLISHED BY THE PRESS SYNDICATE OF THE UNIVERSITY OF CAMBRIDGE
The Pitt Building, Trumpington Street, Cambridge, United Kingdom

CAMBRIDGE UNIVERSITY PRESS
The Edinburgh Building, Cambridge CB2 2RU, UK
40 West 20th Street, New York, NY 10011–4211, USA
477 Williamstown Road, Port Melbourne, VIC 3207, Australia
Ruiz de Alarcón 13, 28014 Madrid, Spain
Dock House, The Waterfront, Cape Town 8001, South Africa

http://www.cambridge.org

© Cambridge University Press 1996

First published 1996
Eighth printing 2003

Printed in the United Kingdom at the University Press, Cambridge

ISBN 0 521 45631 2 Personal Study Workbook
ISBN 0 521 45632 0 Class Book
ISBN 0 521 45630 4 Teacher's Book
ISBN 0 521 45629 0 Class Cassette Set
ISBN 0 521 45628 2 Personal Study Workbook Cassette
ISBN 0 521 48576 2 Personal Study Workbook Audio CD

# CONTENTS

# LOOKING BACK AND LOOKING FORWARD

## 1 Words with similar meanings

**A** Look at the words in the left-hand box and find words with a similar meaning in the right-hand box.

Example: boring *is similar to* dull.

| | | |
|---|---|---|
| great | scared stiff | upset |
| worried | relaxed | nervous |
| awful | boring | huge |

| | | | |
|---|---|---|---|
| calm | terrific | dreadful | tense |
| dull | terrified | enormous | |
| anxious | unhappy | | |

**B** We often use words with similar meaning to repeat what someone has said.

Examples:  A: I thought the film was boring.
            B: Yes, it was very dull.

            A: It was enormous, wasn't it?
            B: Yes, huge.

Respond to these sentences in a similar way. Use a word with a similar meaning in each one.

1. Are you feeling nervous?
2. I was scared stiff, weren't you?
3. It's an awful restaurant, isn't it?
4. I thought he looked quite worried, didn't you?
5. Is she still unhappy about it?
6. Do those pills make you feel calmer?
7. I thought it was a great book, didn't you?
8. That man at the party was very dull, wasn't he?

## 2 Something's missing here

**A** Each of these past tense forms has a letter missing. Complete the verbs. Be careful: sometimes there is more than one possibility.

Examples:         _ut         _tole
         Answers: *put* or *cut*    *stole*

| | | | | | | | | |
|---|---|---|---|---|---|---|---|---|
| _eard | _ound | _aw | _ought | _hrew | _urt | _aught | _ore | _ost |
| _hose | _new | _ent | _it | _lept | _on | _pent | _lew | _old |

**B** Now complete these sentences.

1. _e _ent _wo _arcels _o _is _rother _or _is _irthday.
2. _he _lane _lew _ery _ow _ver _ur _eads.
3. _y _eacher _aught _e _verything I _now.
4. _ast _eek _ou _old _e _our _ister _as _ll.
5. _he _inner _ost _ore _han _he _ad.
6. _he _eam _on _he _ootball _atch, _ut _ost _he _up.

Put the words in the box onto the diagrams in a suitable place.

| diet    bed and breakfast    gardening    van    season ticket    loan |
| weight training    jewellery    cottage    drawing    tracksuit    wallet |
| sunbathing    bungalow    parking space    bill    diary    credit card |

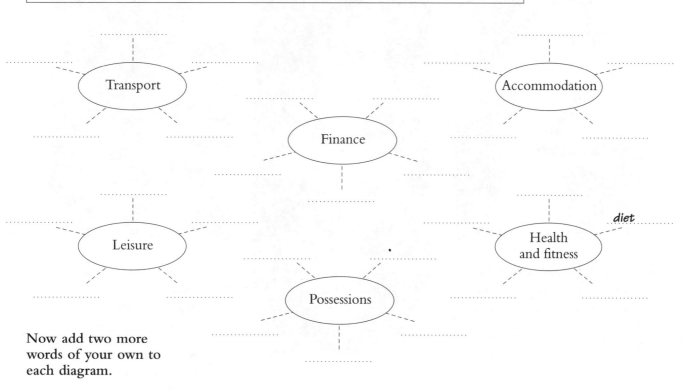

Now add two more
words of your own to
each diagram.

**A** Match words from the left with words from the right to form 12 compound nouns.

| | |
|---|---|
| traffic | teeth |
| primary | meter |
| central | conditioning |
| zebra | card |
| false | machine |
| income | heating |
| air | crossing |
| post | tax |
| parking | disc |
| credit | office |
| car | jam |
| washing | school |
| compact | park |

**B** With compound words it is important to know which part has the main stress.

Example: *car park, but compact disc*

It is more common to have the main stress on the first word, but you may need to
check the stress with your teacher or a dictionary. Unfortunately, some dictionaries do
not mark the stress on compound words.

⫼ Look at the compound words above. Mark the main stress, and then listen to the
recording to check your answers. After that, practise saying the words with the recording.

---

Read the texts and answer the questions.

If actor **Michael J Fox** ever shows signs of letting all the success and adulation go to his head, there's always his family to bring him back down to earth.

'I'll never forget when I won my first Emmy award,' Fox says. 'I flew home with it to show my family and proudly put it on the hall table. The next day, my brother's boxing trophy, my mother's bowling trophy and my father's bridge trophy were all sitting next to it. And no one said a word.'

Prima ballerina **Margot Fonteyn** remembers her first dance step:

'I was just three years old and we were living in the London suburb of Ealing. In the house there was a staircase. One day while I was playing I slipped or jumped down four or five steps. I don't know why I did it, but the fact is I had the marvellous sensation of having flown like a bird, or a butterfly, or like a fairy, perhaps.

I can tell you that however often I tried afterwards, I was never able to recapture that unforgettable first dance step.'

**Jackie Joyner-Kersee**, US Olympic gold heptathlon champion, learnt a lot of important qualities – modesty, faith and perseverance – from her mother.

'She was just a child herself, bringing up another child,' Jackie says. 'My mother wanted to protect me. I couldn't wear flashy clothes or go out with boys until I was 18. We were so poor that I never asked for anything; instead, I put all my interest in school and sport.'

The pride that her mother helped her to develop meant that she finished in the top 10% in her class, and set a record for the long jump.

'I never lost hope,' says Jackie. 'I always had something to aim for. I kept telling myself: you have to work hard; you have to be successful.'

Whose memories are these, do you think?

1. My family helped me.
2. I knew how it felt to fly.
3. I had a strict childhood.
4. I did well because I forced myself to improve.
5. My early experience changed my life.
6. You need someone to help you put your life in perspective.

Which story do you like most? Tell your speaking partner next time you speak to them.

Listen to these people recalling recent historical events. Complete the table with any four events for each year.

| 1981 | 1985 | 1989 |
|------|------|------|
| 1. ................................ | ................................ | ................................ |
| 2. ................................ | ................................ | ................................ |
| 3. ................................ | ................................ | ................................ |
| 4. ................................ | ................................ | ................................ |

Read the letter, then complete it using the verbs in the box in the correct form. Use the present simple, past simple, present continuous or *will* + infinitive.

| try | know | move | be | start | pack | think | find | enjoy |
|-----|------|------|-----|-------|------|-------|------|-------|
| see | live | have | | | | | | |

> 19, Elverton Hill,
> Leamington,
> Warwickshire
>
> 14th June
>
> Dear Joe,
>
> This is just to let you know that we ........................ house next week, on Friday to be exact. Our new address ........................ :
>
> 14, Howards Cottages,
> Leamington, Warwickshire
> Tel: 330041
>
> As you ........................, we first ........................ looking for a larger house with a garden about six months ago. We ........................ (not) anything we liked for a long time, but about two months ago, we ........................ a really pretty cottage with a fantastic garden, very near the flat we ........................ in at the moment. I really ........................ we ........................ living there very much.
>
> Of course we are very busy: Tom ........................ to sort out all his clothes and sports equipment, and I ........................ all the kitchen things. What a mess!
>
> By the way, we ........................ a party at our new home on Saturday the 29th, with some of our new and old neighbours. Do come.
>
> See you soon.
>
> Love,
>
> Penny

Now write a letter to your teacher or your speaking partner. In it, tell him or her any of the following:

– something you did last week, last weekend or yesterday
– something you are doing temporarily, but not necessarily at the moment of writing
– an arrangement you have made for the future
– something you predict or believe will happen soon.

## 8 Speaking partners

A speaking partner is someone you can practise your English with outside class. Agree to meet regularly at a certain time in a certain place to practise speaking English together. If you cannot meet for any reason, you can still talk to your speaking partner on the telephone. Throughout this book you will find ideas for things you can talk about with your speaking partner.

In Review and Development in the Class Book, you looked at ways of revising. One way was to work with a partner and test each other.

Use this method with your speaking partner. Try the following:

**Class Book**
1. Look at the vocabulary on page 7. Give your partner a word and ask them to explain it or give a translation.
2. Read a short passage aloud to each other. For example, the two short texts on technology and transport on page 8. If possible, record them and then listen together. Can you hear any pronunciation mistakes?
3. Ask your partner if they can remember:
   − three different uses of the present continuous
   − different ways of revising things (from Review and Development).

**Personal Study Workbook**
4. Ask your partner to read the compound nouns in Exercise 4 on page 5 with the correct word stress.
5. Test your partner on the irregular verbs in Exercise 2, or any from the irregular verb list on page 155. You say the infinitive form, your partner should say the past tense form.
6. Tell your partner which reading text you liked most in Exercise 5, and why.
7. Show your partner what you wrote in Exercise 7.

Now discuss which kind of revision you find most useful to do together.

## 9 Visual dictionary

Complete the visual dictionary for Unit 1 on page 116.

## 10 Reflections

This space is for you to make a note of things you have learnt in this unit. You can also use it as a diary to write about your problems and progress in English.

..............................................................................................................................................

..............................................................................................................................................

..............................................................................................................................................

..............................................................................................................................................

..............................................................................................................................................

..............................................................................................................................................

..............................................................................................................................................

..............................................................................................................................................

..............................................................................................................................................

..............................................................................................................................................

# HOW DOES THAT SOUND?

**1 Hair or hairs?**                                       uncountable nouns

Correct any mistakes in these sentences. Be careful: some of them have no mistakes.

1. Could you pass me today's papers? I haven't had a chance to read them yet.
2. I need a clean paper to write on.
3. She's doing some medical researches at the moment.
4. All of you can find accommodation through the school.
5. I didn't think much of their advices, did you?
6. Have you brought all the sports equipments?
7. We haven't got enough room in the car to take them with us.
8. There have been many times when I have thought of leaving, but as you can see, I'm still here.
9. Have you got any previous experiences of selling washing machines, Mr Turville?
10. I've got lots of luggage – we'd better take a taxi.
11. We need some more informations about that.
12. She owns a small shop which sells antique furnitures.

**2 Much more interesting than I thought**          comparative and superlative structures

Complete the sentences using an appropriate adjective and one of the structures below.

**Comparative**
*a bit* (adjective + *-er*) *than* …
Examples: *a bit hotter than, a bit longer than*
*much, far* or *a great deal* (*more* + adjective) *than* …
Example: *much more interesting than*
**Superlative**
*the* (adjective + *-est*)
Examples: *the hottest, the longest*
or
*the* (*most* + adjective)
Example: *the most interesting*

Example: *Motor bikes* <u>are much more expensive than</u> *bicycles.*
         *The Sahara* <u>is the largest</u> *desert in the world.*

1. Gold .......................................... silver.

2. Fishing .......................................... athletics.

3. Boxing .......................................... sport in the world.

4. Girls .......................................... boys.

5. Pronunciation .......................................... grammar.

6. The Nile .......................................... in the world.

7. The North Pole .......................................... the South Pole.

8. Writing by hand .......................................... typing.

9. Food .......................................... thing in my life.

10. Photographs .......................................... drawings.

Next time you see your speaking partner, compare your answers.

If the opposite of *the biggest* is *the smallest*, and the opposite of *the most expensive* is *the cheapest*, what is the opposite of the following?

|  | *Opposite* |
|---|---|
| 1. The largest city | ................................................. |
| 2. The most dangerous place | ................................................. |
| 3. The best singer | ................................................. |
| 4. The youngest person | ................................................. |
| 5. The most beautiful view | ................................................. |
| 6. The most careless drivers | ................................................. |
| 7. The greatest actor | ................................................. |
| 8. The shortest man | ................................................. |
| 9. The shortest river | ................................................. |
| 10. The most difficult question | ................................................. |
| 11. The meanest person | ................................................. |
| 12. The most stupid student | ................................................. |
| 13. The lightest room | ................................................. |
| 14. The lightest suitcase | ................................................. |
| 15. The wildest animal | ................................................. |
| 16. The strongest coffee | ................................................. |
| 17. The strongest cigarettes | ................................................. |
| 18. The most horrible person | ................................................. |
| 19. The most competitive group | ................................................. |
| 20. The most | ................................................. |

Complete the sentences with suitable words from the box. In some cases you must change the adjective in the box (e.g. *soft*) into an adverb (e.g. *softly*).

| soft | loud | irritating | easy | calm | clear | reliable | distinctive |
|---|---|---|---|---|---|---|---|
| charming | attractive | quick | deep | cheerful | quiet | reassuring | |

1. I understood the lesson because she pronounced everything very

    ................................................. Our other teacher sometimes speaks very

    ................................................, so he's more difficult to understand.

2. The boy kept shouting in a ................................................. voice. I expect they could hear

    him in the next street.

3. It helps politicians and actors if they have a ................................................. voice because

    people will then remember them more .................................................

4. I find it very ................................................. when people mumble all the time.

5. She's got such a ............................................... voice that some people think she sounds like a man.

6. It was a tense situation and everyone was extremely nervous, but he got up and spoke in a very ............................................... way and that really helped to relax people.

7. I don't know why he was so happy, but when I saw him he was whistling ............................................... and looking very pleased with himself.

8. She bent down and whispered ............................................... in his ear.

9. He's a good member of the football team. He's very ............................................... – he comes to all the training sessions.

In syllables that are not stressed, some vowels (particularly 'a' and 'o') are often pronounced /ə/. This is very common if the vowel is in a syllable directly before or after a stressed syllable, but it sometimes happens in other syllables as well.

📼 Listen to the examples on the recording.

Examples: *Brazil*   *policeman*   *magazine*

Where does the sound /ə/ appear in these words? Use a dictionary to check.

| | | | | | |
|---|---|---|---|---|---|
| Japan | machine | certificate | professor | reliable | career |
| comfortable | photographer | Arabic | weather | Italy | accommodation |

📼 Repeat the sentences you hear on the recording.

**A** If you were deaf, which of the following situations might be a problem for you?

1. Someone comes to your front door.
2. You are using your oven.
3. Someone rings you up.
4. You are in town, crossing the road.
5. You have to wake up at a certain time in the morning.
6. You are in a public building when a fire alarm goes off.

**B** You probably know about guide dogs for blind people, but have you ever heard of hearing dogs for the deaf?

Read the text and see which of the situations in Exercise A are mentioned.

1 *P*auline Stark no longer jumps when people walk up behind her. Friends don't go away disappointed because she hasn't heard them at the door, and she doesn't ignore the timer on her oven and burn her dinner. These things used to happen before Frisky, her intelligent and highly trained hearing dog, entered her life.

2 Frisky's training was paid for with the help of the staff at the Marks and Spencer store in Oxford, as part of the company's community involvement programme. Training costs about £2,500 and Pauline feels this money is well spent. 'The problem is that people can see someone is blind, but they don't understand deafness. Even if you explain to them you need to lip-read, they still turn their faces away when they talk,' says Pauline.

3 'I don't know how I managed without Frisky. She's very good at letting me know when the phone rings, or when there's someone at the door.'

4 *T*ony Blunt is a former police-dog handler who retired early to establish Hearing Dogs for the Deaf in 1982. Many of the dogs that are trained come from rescue centres and Tony may spend up to a year deciding whether the dog is suitable or not. It then spends 16 weeks at a training centre where it is taught to respond to certain sounds such as alarm clocks, telephones, fire alarms, etc. Dogs are taught to put their feet on the bed to wake the person when the alarm goes off, or to run up to the person and touch them before taking them to the source of the sound. The exception is the fire alarm. 'In this case,' says Tony, 'we teach the dog to attract attention and then lie down.'

5 Tony stresses that the benefits are much deeper than allowing the person to respond to bells and buzzers. 'When people lose their hearing, they often lose their confidence as well and want to shut themselves away. Having the dogs gets them out, and ends the feelings of loneliness and isolation.'

**C** These four parts of sentences have been taken from the text. Where should they go?

... although some are donated by breeders (paragraph 4)
... and like all hearing dogs, she's very nosy! (paragraph 3)
... (the same model as that belonging to the dog's future owner) (paragraph 4)
... that most people who can hear never even think about (paragraph 4)

📟 Listen to the extracts on the recording. Where would you hear them, and what are the messages about?

Complete the table.

| | Where | Messages |
|---|---|---|
| 1. | .................................................. | .................................................. |
| 2. | .................................................. | .................................................. |
| 3. | .................................................. | .................................................. |
| 4. | .................................................. | .................................................. |
| 5. | .................................................. | .................................................. |

## 8 Sound story                                                writing

Look at the picture and read the beginning of the story.

It was a terrible, windy night in the middle of winter, and I was at home one evening, sitting in front of the fire. Suddenly I heard ...

📟 Listen to the sounds on the recording, and write the rest of the story.

## 9 Speaking partners

Choose some of the questions below to discuss together.

1. What sounds do you associate with the following?
   - a festival in your town/country
   - a season: spring, summer, autumn or winter
   - family occasions/celebrations
   - late evening where you live
   - early morning where you live
   - your workplace
2. Which sounds do you particularly like or dislike?

3. If you have read the text about hearing dogs in Exercise 6:
   Do you think people have the right to use animals at all?
   Is it right for humans to use animals for medical research?
   Is it right to use them to test cosmetics?
   Is it right for the police to use dogs to help catch criminals?
   Is it right to use them to sniff for drugs?
   Is it right to use dogs for hunting?
   Is it right to use them as companions?
4. What answers did you give to Exercise 2 in this unit of the Personal Study Workbook?


## 10 Visual dictionary

Complete the visual dictionary for Unit 2 on page 117.


## 11 Reflections

This space is for you to make a note of things you have learnt in this unit. You can also
use it as a diary to write about your problems and progress in English.

..........................................................................................................................
..........................................................................................................................
..........................................................................................................................
..........................................................................................................................
..........................................................................................................................
..........................................................................................................................
..........................................................................................................................
..........................................................................................................................
..........................................................................................................................
..........................................................................................................................
..........................................................................................................................
..........................................................................................................................
..........................................................................................................................
..........................................................................................................................

# 3

# GAMES PEOPLE PLAY

Complete the texts using an *-ing* form or infinitive. Then decide what sport or game is being described in each text.

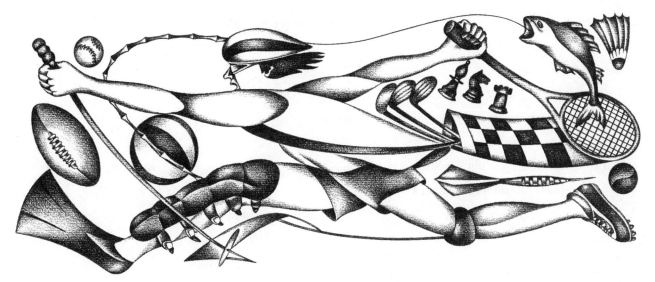

A

With this sport, it's difficult to avoid ............................................ (spend) a lot of money. In many places you have to join a club, and they sometimes refuse ............................................ (accept) you. Then there is the cost of the equipment, which is also very high. You can learn ............................................ (play) it quite quickly, but you'll spend years ............................................ (try) to perfect your technique: especially the swing!

B

It's difficult to imagine ............................................ (do) this sport if you're middle-aged: it really seems to be a young person's sport because you need ............................................ (be) physically very fit. There isn't much expense involved but you need a good pair of trainers. You should start ............................................ (do) it as young as possible. If you can't stand ............................................ (get up) early and training hard in the open air on winter mornings, this isn't the sport for you.

C

This is a game which is very popular in Russia and the Ukraine, but people from many countries are interested in either ............................................ (play) or ............................................ (watch). And you can enjoy ............................................ (play) it at any age as it's a game of mental skill. If you want ............................................ (take) part in competitions, however, it's a demanding business. If you can manage ............................................ (persuade) someone ............................................ (buy) you a board and pieces at an early age, you'll get off to a good start. You may even become a grand champion.

Complete the sentences with a word from the left and a preposition from the right.

| afraid | depend | good | | in | on | of | at | about |
|---|---|---|---|---|---|---|---|---|
| worried | proud | shy | fear | | | | | |
| interested | point | kind | | | | | | |

1. My brother is very ......................................... ................ tennis and has won several

   championships, but I've never been ......................................... ............. sport.

2. I was ......................................... ................ heights when I was younger.

3. I'm ......................................... ................ my son: he's planning to start parachute

   jumping this year.

4. Football fans are ......................................... ............... the teams they support.

5. I go skiing most weekends in the winter, but obviously it ...............................

   .................... the weather.

6. I'm an Olympic athlete but I'm still very ......................................... ............. speaking

   in public when I'm interviewed on TV.

7. If you have a ......................................... ............... flying, it makes international travel

   very difficult.

8. A saddle is a ......................................... ............... seat you put on a horse.

9. I don't really see the ......................................... ............. doing a lot of exercise. It just

   makes you eat more!

When a word ends in a consonant and the next word starts with a vowel, the two
words are usually joined together. For example:

*She took it off.*
*Four eggs, please.*
*How much is a cup of coffee?*

It is this feature of English which sometimes makes it difficult to distinguish individual
words and understand spoken English.

☐☐ Listen and write down the sentences you hear on the recording, and check your
answers with the tapescript.

1. .................................................................................................................

2. .................................................................................................................

3. .................................................................................................................

4. .................................................................................................................

5. .................................................................................................................

6. .................................................................................................................

7. .................................................................................................................

8. .................................................................................................................

Now draw lines (as in the examples) to show which words are joined together in spoken
English. Listen to the recording again, and practise saying the sentences in the same way.

## 4 Full of skill, or skilful?

**A** Complete the table.

| Nouns | Adjectives | Nouns | Adjectives |
|---|---|---|---|
| _boredom_ | boring/bored | ................... | shy |
| ................... | confident | ................... | frightening/frightened |
| ................... | skilful | ................... | optimistic |
| ................... | competitive | ................... | knowledgeable |
| ................... | interesting/interested | | |

**B** ▭ Now listen to the recording. You will hear eight people being described. For each description, complete a sentence below using an appropriate word from the table.

Example: 1. *Joe is* _bored._ ...........................

2. Sue is ................................. .

3. Mark is ................................. .

4. Jane is ................................. .

5. Marta is ................................. .

6. Lino has ................................. .

7. Alana suffers from ................................. .

8. Julian has a lot of ................................. .

## 5 Women are catching up

Read the text and answer the questions.

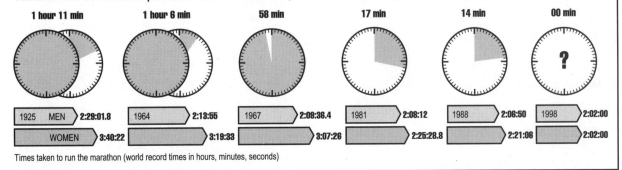

# WOMEN ARE CATCHING UP

A study of Olympic track events this century by two academics has revealed that women are improving so rapidly that in the future they could match the best that Carl Lewis achieved in his prime.

Professor Brian Whipp and Professor Susan Ward, physiologists working at the University of California, have found that women are on course to catch up with male athletes in the marathon in a little over six years. And if present rates of improvement are sustained, they could equal men in other track events before 2050.

Suggested reasons for this progress are greater participation by women in athletics, better technology, and a much greater commitment to training than in the past – women are now as dedicated and competitive as their male counterparts. Sadly, a further reason for this progress has been the illegal use of drugs, especially in the 70s and 80s. However, since routine drug testing has become a feature of men's and women's athletics, the use of drugs has declined, but so have the performances in some women's events, particularly the power events such as the shot putt. The same is true of some men's events as well, but not to quite the same extent.

There are those who believe that women will never catch up men. Dr Ron Maughan, a senior lecturer at Aberdeen University Medical School, who specialises in physiology and the biochemistry of exercise, says that 'men tend to be bigger and stronger, they tend to have better hearts and lungs, and more men take part in sport.'

Bookmakers seem to agree with Dr Maughan. A leading firm of bookmakers will currently give odds of 500–1 against a woman holding the world marathon record by the year 2000, and the same odds against a woman holding the 100m record by the year 2050. Even women athletes usually agree with this analysis. Liz McColgan, world champion at 10,000 metres in 1991, believes that the gap could be narrowed, but that a woman will never beat the best man because of the difference in physique.

**CLOSING THE GAP: The stopwatches show the difference, in world record times, between male and female marathon runners**

| 1 hour 11 min | 1 hour 6 min | 58 min | 17 min | 14 min | 00 min |
|---|---|---|---|---|---|

| 1925 | MEN | 2:29:01.8 | 1964 | 2:13:55 | 1967 | 2:09:36.4 | 1981 | 2:08:12 | 1988 | 2:06:50 | 1998 | 2:02:00 |
| | WOMEN | 3:40:22 | | 3:19:33 | | 3:07:26 | | 2:25:28.8 | | 2:21:06 | | 2:02:00 |

Times taken to run the marathon (world record times in hours, minutes, seconds)

1. Write down three reasons why women are getting better at athletics.

   ........................................................................................

   ........................................................................................

   ........................................................................................

2. Write down three reasons why women might never equal men in athletics events.

   ........................................................................................

   ........................................................................................

   ........................................................................................

   ........................................................................................

3. Which of these sentences best summarises the article:
   a. Men will always be far superior to women in athletics events.
   b. Men will always be superior, but the difference between men and women will get smaller and smaller.
   c. Men are superior now and the difference between men and women will grow.
   d. Women will eventually equal men in athletics events.

## 6  What does that mean?                                   writing: paraphrase

Imagine someone in your English class asked you to explain some words. Write down what you would say, and try to use some of the phrases on page 23 of the Class Book.

Example: A: *What does* key *mean?*
          YOUR ANSWER: *It's a thing you use for locking a door.*

1. What does *can't stand* mean?

   ........................................................................................

2. What's a *casino*?

   ........................................................................................

3. What is a *contestant*?

   ........................................................................................

4. What does *referee* mean?

   ........................................................................................

5. What's a *track*?

   ........................................................................................

6. What does *afraid* mean?

   ........................................................................................

7. What's a *ladder*?

   ........................................................................................

8. What's a *racket*?

   ........................................................................................

9. What's *toothpaste*?

   ........................................................................................

## 7 Speaking partners

**A** Look at the vocabulary from any of the first three units of the Class Book or from the visual dictionary, and test each other by giving paraphrases as on page 8 in the Class Book.

Example: A: *It's something you put your clothes in when you go on holiday.*
B: *Your suitcase?*
A: *Nearly – it means all your suitcases and bags.*
B: *Oh, you mean luggage.*
A: *That's right.*

**B** Choose any of these topics and discuss them.

1. Sport and leisure interests of anyone in your family.
2. A recent sporting event you both saw or read about (for example, a football or tennis match, a sumo contest, an international championship).
3. (If you come from different countries) the most popular sport or leisure activities in your countries. Say why they are popular.
4. The benefits of sport and the problems it can cause.

## 8 Visual dictionary

Complete the visual dictionary for Unit 3 on page 118.

## 9 Reflections

This space is for you to make a note of things you have learnt in this unit. You can also use it as a diary to write about your problems and progress in English.

........................................................................................
........................................................................................
........................................................................................
........................................................................................
........................................................................................
........................................................................................
........................................................................................
........................................................................................
........................................................................................
........................................................................................
........................................................................................
........................................................................................
........................................................................................
........................................................................................
........................................................................................

# NEWSPAPERS AND MAGAZINES

Respond to these sentences with a question using *How long* + past simple or *How long* + present perfect. Which one you use will depend on the sentence.

Examples:   A: *I lived in Rome when I was a child.*
B: *How long* <u>did you live there</u> ?
A: *I'm working for a theatre company.*
B: *How long* <u>have you worked there</u> ?

1. I used to have a beautiful old Peugeot.

..............................................................................................

2. I live with my sister in Madrid.

..............................................................................................

3. I've got a terrible cold.

..............................................................................................

4. I first met my husband at a party.

..............................................................................................

5. I enjoyed my English course in New York.

..............................................................................................

6. I wear contact lenses.

..............................................................................................

7. I've shaved off my beard.

..............................................................................................

8. I never eat meat.

..............................................................................................

Complete the text with words from the box.

> tabloid newspapers    journalists    international news    broadsheets    scoop
> print    circulation figures    articles    home news    reporters    editors
> copies    headlines

After the Second World War, newspapers in Britain became more polarised into two

extremes: the quality press, mainly in the form of (1) ...................................................., and

the popular press, also known as (2) ............................................... . Clearly, the popular

press have very much higher (3) ............................................... and their

(4) ............................................... and (5) ............................................... spend much

time and money looking for a big (6) ............................................... for their front pages.

(7)............................................ are often in very large (8)............................................

and the (9)............................................ in these papers tend to be short, with a lot of

colour photographs. They also have lotteries which are very popular.

At the other end of the scale, the quality press tend to devote much more of their newspapers

to (10)............................................ and (11)............................................. They sell

fewer (12)............................................ and their readership profile is different from that

of the popular press.

All newspaper (13)............................................ have to answer to the Press Complaints

Commission if they publish stories which are untrue.

**Complete the networks with these words.**

| | | | | | |
|---|---|---|---|---|---|
| circulation | cancer | article | shareholder | subscription | profit |
| drugs | invest | company | scandal | treatment | column | revenue |
| editor | suffer | diagnose | sales | illness | | |

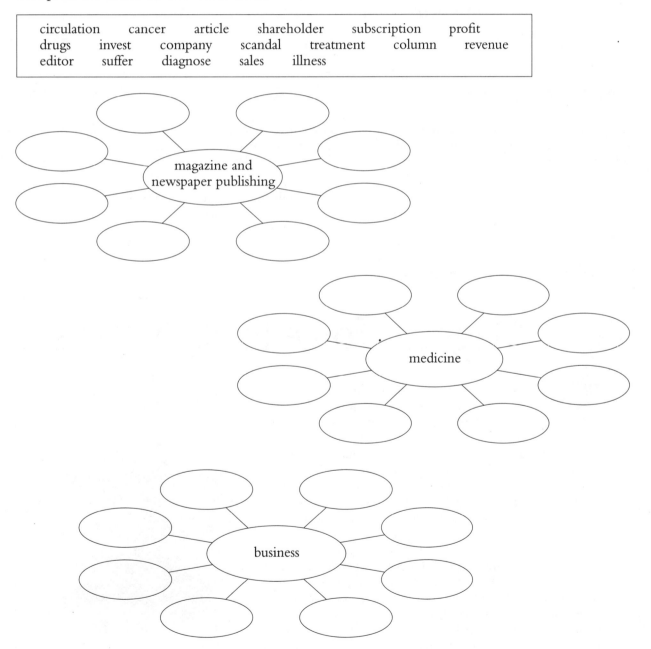

**Now add two more words to each topic.**

## 4 When and where?

Complete the text with words from the box.

| during | in | since | at | by | on | for |
|---|---|---|---|---|---|---|

I arrived (1)..................... May last year, and (2)..................... the end of the year I spoke
quite good English. (3)..................... first it was very difficult, of course, and
(4)..................... the summer I spent a lot of time with other Italians so my English didn't
improve a lot; but (5)..................... the end of August I haven't spoken much Italian because
most of my friends come from France or Germany or Japan. I love travelling around, so
(6)..................... Christmas I went to Scotland (7)..................... ten days, and
(8)..................... a couple weeks I'm going (9)..................... holiday with a few friends.
We are going to stay (10)..................... a little cottage (11)..................... the coast, and that
will be very nice because I haven't been to the seaside (12)..................... two years
(13)..................... least.

## 5 *Women & Guns*

The article is about a magazine in America for women who own guns. Before you read
the article, look at this list of words and phrases. How many do you think will appear
in the article? Use a dictionary to help you.

| pistol | victim | rape | shower | security | violence | scared | a will |
|---|---|---|---|---|---|---|---|
| shoot | illegal | wild | self-defence | election | skirt | actress | |
| weapon | | | | | | | |

Read the text and check if your guesses were correct.

# Magnum Force In High Heels

*Women & Guns* is published in Washington State, and
started when its editor, Sonny Jones, still lived in
Atlanta. Working in the jewellery business, she felt
she was a potential victim. 'I became very security-
conscious and one thing I did was to carry a gun.' But then she
discovered that 'people who taught gunhandling didn't take
women seriously'. So she founded the *Women & Guns* magazine
with the help of the Second Amendment Foundation, an
organisation dedicated to preserving the Second Amendment: the
right to carry arms.

When it was first published in 1989, the magazine was sold by
subscription only; now it is available nationwide, its circulation
is growing and over 80% of its readers own a gun. This is not
really surprising. In the US where violence is widespread,
women are scared, and lots of scared women want guns.
According to *The Washington Post*, at least 12 million women in the US
legally own guns, and maybe another 15 million more are considering the idea.

The magazine is full of technical information about guns, as well as product advice, profiles of champion women shooters and letters from the editor, Ms Jones. Legal advice is also provided. Karen MacNutt, a consulting lawyer for gun groups, advises women who are getting a divorce to give their guns to friends, not the authorities, for safekeeping. If they do there is no danger they will kill their husband. Then, when the 'emotion leaves the divorce' they can get their weapon back without applying to the authorities.

The magazine also includes book reviews and information about places where women can meet together and practise. And it is full of useful tips for women who are carrying a gun. 'Some women wear an ankle holster with evening wear! This won't work if the long formal skirt has a slit in the back – you wouldn't be able to walk without having it show – and of course the dress must be quite long so that the holster won't show through the fabric while you're dancing or watching the opera.'

**Answer these questions.**

1. Why did Sonny Jones decide to carry a gun?
2. How did she first sell her new magazine?
3. How many women in the United States have a gun?
4. Does the magazine give information about the law and guns?
5. Why do they suggest women who are getting a divorce should give their gun to a friend?
6. What is the problem for women who wear guns in the evening?

## 6 What do you read?

▢ Listen to these people talking about magazines they read. Fill in the table.

|  | *What do they read?* | *Why?* |
|---|---|---|
| Speaker 1 | .................................. | .................................. |
| Speaker 2 | .................................. | .................................. |
| Speaker 3 | .................................. | .................................. |
| Speaker 4 | .................................. | .................................. |

## 7 Personal questionnaire

Magazines often print questionnaires completed by famous people. Here is one from an English paper. Complete it about yourself.

| | | | |
|---|---|---|---|
| **1.** | What objects do you always carry with you? | **7.** | Who or what is the greatest love of your life? |
| **2.** | What is your favourite smell? | **8.** | Which living person do you most admire? |
| **3.** | What is your favourite English word? | **9.** | Which living person do you most dislike? |
| **4.** | What is your favourite building? | **10.** | On what occasions do you tell lies? |
| **5.** | What is your favourite journey? | **11.** | What single thing would most improve the quality of your life? |
| **6.** | What is your greatest fear? | **12.** | Which talent would you most like to have? |

## 8 Speaking partners

**A** Discuss your answers to Exercise 7 with your partner.

**B** Practise Exercise 1 with your partner as a dialogue.

**C** Choose any of these questions to discuss:

1. When you read a newspaper, which section do you read first, and why?
2. Which sections do you never read? Why not?
3. Do you always read the same paper? Why / why not?
4. If you are from different countries, tell your partner what daily papers are sold in your country, and what you think of them.
5. What do you think of the press in your country? Do you think they do a good job?
6. Who owns the press in your country?

## 9 Reflections

This space is for you to make a note of things you have learnt in this unit. You can also use it as a diary to write about your problems and progress in English.

........................................................................................................................................
........................................................................................................................................
........................................................................................................................................
........................................................................................................................................
........................................................................................................................................
........................................................................................................................................
........................................................................................................................................
........................................................................................................................................
........................................................................................................................................
........................................................................................................................................
........................................................................................................................................
........................................................................................................................................
........................................................................................................................................

Unit 4 NEWSPAPERS AND MAGAZINES

# 5

# RELATIONSHIPS

Decide whether these sentences are true or false. Correct any that are false.

1. If you are married, you may have a father-in-law and mother-in-law.
2. If your brother is married, his wife is your sister.
3. If your mother remarried and had a boy, he would be your stepson.
4. Your aunt could be your mother's sister, or your father's sister.
5. Your cousins are the children of your brothers and sisters.
6. Your nephew could be your brother's son or your sister's son.
7. If you have two uncles, they must be men.
8. Your uncles and aunts are your parents.
9. Your grandmother could be your mother's mother or your father's mother.
10. If you are a woman you can't have a niece.

## 2 *Ships* and *hoods*         word building: suffixes

**A** Some nouns can be changed to other nouns by adding the suffixes *-ship* or *-hood*.

Examples:   *Friend**ship** is the state or experience of being friends.*
           *Mother**hood** is the state of being a mother.*

Which of these words take the suffix *-ship* and which take *-hood*?

| | | | | | | |
|---|---|---|---|---|---|---|
| partner | relation | father | leader | parent | dictator | adult |
| member | apprentice | child | | | | |

**B** Use the words you have formed to complete these sentences.

1. Two people working together in an equal relationship are in a ..................................... .

2. ..................................... is the state you reach after adolescence.

3. An ..................................... is the period of training when a person learns a particular skill for a job.

4. ..................................... is a state which carries great responsibility because it involves looking after children.

5. ..................................... is an important quality for prime ministers and politicians.

6. When the ruler of a country has total power, we say that the country is a ..................................... .

7. A connection between two people, for example, a brother and sister, or a doctor and patient, is called a ..................................... .

8. ..................................... is when you belong to a club or organisation.

Complete these sentences and make your own predictions about the future.

1. In ten years' time I will definitely ...................................................
...................................................... .

2. My hair will probably ..................................................................
...................................................... .

3. As far as work is concerned, I'm likely to .....................................
...................................................... .

4. My English is likely to ...............................................................
...................................................... .

5. I might .................................................................................... .

6. In my private life I doubt if ........................................................
...................................................... .

7. My weight is unlikely to .............................................................
...................................................... .

8. In the next ten years, I definitely won't .......................................
...................................................... .

Using the same expressions (*probably*, *definitely*, *likely*, *unlikely*, etc.), write at least four more sentences of your own and show them to your speaking partner.

**A** 📼 Look at the example dialogue, then listen to the recording and repeat the conversation in the spaces. Pay attention to the underlined sounds.

Example: A: *What'<u>s</u> your fa<u>th</u>er'<u>s</u> name?*
         B: *My fa<u>th</u>er? Hi<u>s</u> name's Chri<u>s</u>topher.*
         A: *What'<u>s</u> your grandmo<u>th</u>er's name?*
         B: *My grandmo<u>th</u>er? Her name'<u>s</u> Mar<u>c</u>ia.*

**B** 📼 Now continue, answering the questions on the recording about yourself. Think about your pronunciation and change the tenses if necessary.

📼 Listen to the recording and complete A and B's family tree.

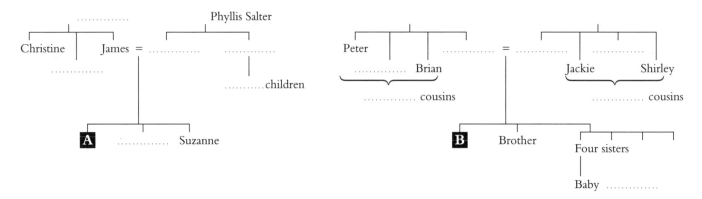

**A** Two couples describe the 'love–hate' relationship they have with their partner. What are A, B, C and D's names? Which of them are couples?

**A**

I adore my wife. Even at this age, and after all those years together, she still means more to me than anyone else in the world. There is something about her that both fascinates and frustrates me at the same time. From the first time I saw her, I was drawn to her. She was very headstrong as a teenager, with dark eyes, and I had the feeling that we were meant for one another in some way. As far as I can remember, most of our arguments were caused by her, simply because she felt like a fight, and enjoyed one. I realised that I was both very lucky and very unlucky to have found a woman who could make me so happy and also unhappy. When we separated I realised I had made a terrible mistake. I did everything I could to win Jill back. I could never be happy with another woman. I know I'm still a terrible husband, I lose my temper easily, and I don't really deserve Jill.

**B**

I really love Alex, but there are times when I want to kill him. There are certain things he does that drive me mad and we end up having terrible rows. You see, I am always making plans for the two of us. Alex never organises anything. He says he appreciates me doing this, but often he forgets what I have arranged. I am hurt because it makes me realise he doesn't pay attention to anything I say. The television is the thing that really divides us. Alex has an awful habit of switching channels every few minutes. I get intensely irritated. And he insists on watching TV to relax rather than going to bed. Then he falls asleep in front of it. Another thing is that he suddenly gets bossy and starts ordering me around. Despite all this, we do have a very good relationship and I just have to accept that there are some things Alex does that will always irritate me.

**C**

At various stages in my life I have probably hated Dan as much as it is possible to hate another human being. But at the same time I know that he is the only man on earth for me. We met when we were both still at school, and I still remember my first impressions of him – very good-looking and funny, but terribly arrogant. I wanted to hit him, but at the same time I also found him impossible to resist. We had our first major fight a month later and we got married soon after. After a few years we got divorced. But I kept thinking of Dan, hoping and yet dreading that I would meet him at a party. I missed the up and down relationship we used to have. I realised we had more fun fighting than most people have being friendly, so we remarried, though we still fight. I suppose I've got used to it now – I can't really imagine living any other way.

**D**

Most of the time, I adore Jane. We have only been together a short time, but already I can't imagine my life without her. I suppose she is the opposite of me in many ways: she is quiet, patient and well-educated whereas I am extrovert, impatient and ignorant. There are times she can drive me half-mad with fury and frustration. She gets very angry with me, and I don't understand what I've done. The more I ask her, the colder and more furious she becomes with me. Sometimes I'm just watching TV, unwinding at the end of a busy day, and she gets furious. I wish she could know what I felt without me having to explain it. Perhaps I have to accept that I will never totally understand her.

**B** Find a word or phrase in the texts with the opposite meaning to the words below.

Example: *hate*          *adore* .............................

fortunate          ...................................................

to ignore          ...................................................

to wake up          ...................................................

ugly          ...................................................

modest          ...................................................

married          ...................................................

to look forward to something          ...................................................

badly-educated          ...................................................

**A** We often use different kinds of pronoun to connect ideas and avoid repetition. Look at the sentences below and use one of the pronouns in the box to replace the words that are crossed out.

| that | there | his | who | which | their | these | them |
|------|-------|-----|-----|-------|-------|-------|------|

Example: *George was a cruel man but ~~George's~~ son was very kind.* (his)

1. Peter and Jill lived in a small village and ~~Peter and Jill's~~ house was right in the centre.

2. There were many books on the table and two of ~~these books~~ belonged to my uncle.

3. He wanted to go out but I didn't think ~~going out~~ was a good idea.

4. She showed me plastic and rubber ones but ~~plastic and rubber ones~~ were all they had.

5. We went to the restaurant. We stayed ~~in the restaurant~~ for about two hours.

6. I took him to the hospital, ~~The hospital~~ has a special wing for asthma patients.

7. He saw a doctor, ~~The doctor~~ gave him some tests.

**B** Now complete the text with suitable reference words.

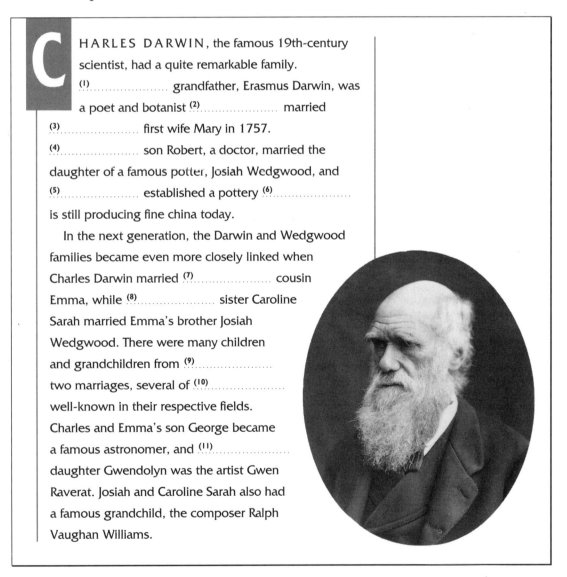

CHARLES DARWIN, the famous 19th-century scientist, had a quite remarkable family.
(1)................... grandfather, Erasmus Darwin, was a poet and botanist (2)................... married (3)................... first wife Mary in 1757. (4)................... son Robert, a doctor, married the daughter of a famous potter, Josiah Wedgwood, and (5)................... established a pottery (6)................... is still producing fine china today.

In the next generation, the Darwin and Wedgwood families became even more closely linked when Charles Darwin married (7)................... cousin Emma, while (8)................... sister Caroline Sarah married Emma's brother Josiah Wedgwood. There were many children and grandchildren from (9)................... two marriages, several of (10)................... well-known in their respective fields. Charles and Emma's son George became a famous astronomer, and (11)................... daughter Gwendolyn was the artist Gwen Raverat. Josiah and Caroline Sarah also had a famous grandchild, the composer Ralph Vaughan Williams.

Write a similar short text about someone in your family from a previous generation, and try to include different reference words.

## 8 Speaking partners

**A** Compare your answers to Exercise 3.

**B** Choose some questions from this questionnaire to discuss with your speaking partner.

1. How important is friendship to you?
   a. Most important of all.   b. Very important.   c. Quite important but not as important as family relationships.   d. Not very important at all.   e. Unimportant.
2. How long have you known your best friend?
3. How often do you see your best friend (or two best friends)?
4. How much do you value the advice of your friends? Would you ask their advice about:
   – a business problem?
   – a problem in your family?
   – a problem with other friends?
5. Which of these statements about friends and friendship do you agree with?
   a. Like good wines, friends become better as you get older.
   b. Your best friends are always the ones you make at school. Later on, you can never get as close to other people.
   c. As you grow older your friends have a different importance to you.
   d. Friendship is never as strong as love.
   e. Friendships can only survive over the years if both friends are prepared to change.
   f. A man and a woman can never really be friends.
   g. Men have stronger friendships with other men than women do with other women.

## 9 Visual dictionary

Complete the visual dictionary for Unit 5 on page 119.

## 10 Reflections

This space is for you to make a note of things you have learnt in this unit. You can also use it as a diary to write about your problems and progress in English.

....................................................................................................................................................

....................................................................................................................................................

....................................................................................................................................................

....................................................................................................................................................

....................................................................................................................................................

....................................................................................................................................................

....................................................................................................................................................

....................................................................................................................................................

....................................................................................................................................................

....................................................................................................................................................

....................................................................................................................................................

....................................................................................................................................................

....................................................................................................................................................

....................................................................................................................................................

# LIFE'S LITTLE CHORES

**1 Diary extract**

past simple and continuous

Put the verbs in brackets into the past simple or past continuous.

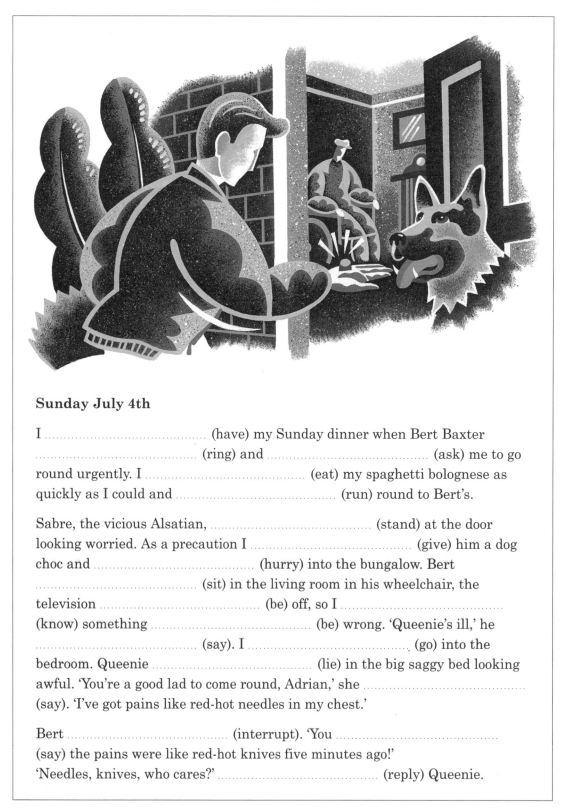

**Sunday July 4th**

I ................................... (have) my Sunday dinner when Bert Baxter
................................... (ring) and ................................... (ask) me to go
round urgently. I ................................... (eat) my spaghetti bolognese as
quickly as I could and ................................... (run) round to Bert's.

Sabre, the vicious Alsatian, ................................... (stand) at the door
looking worried. As a precaution I ................................... (give) him a dog
choc and ................................... (hurry) into the bungalow. Bert
................................... (sit) in the living room in his wheelchair, the
television ................................... (be) off, so I ...................................
(know) something ................................... (be) wrong. 'Queenie's ill,' he
................................... (say). I ................................... (go) into the
bedroom. Queenie ................................... (lie) in the big saggy bed looking
awful. 'You're a good lad to come round, Adrian,' she ...................................
(say). 'I've got pains like red-hot needles in my chest.'

Bert ................................... (interrupt). 'You ...................................
(say) the pains were like red-hot knives five minutes ago!'
'Needles, knives, who cares?' ................................... (reply) Queenie.

Unit 6 LIFE'S LITTLE CHORES

Match the verbs on the left with the
nouns on the right.

| | |
|---|---|
| plug in | a suitcase |
| light | a present |
| get off | my arms |
| spill | a TV |
| pack | a fire |
| wrap up | a bus |
| fasten | a queue |
| go out | my foot |
| jump | a jacket |
| do up | coffee |
| fold | a seat belt |
| hurt | with friends |

Write down the things you have done this week on the left, and the things you haven't
done this week on the right.

Examples: *I've plugged in a TV.*     *I haven't lit a fire.*

*Have done this week*                                *Haven't done this week*

......................................................     ......................................................

......................................................     ......................................................

......................................................     ......................................................

......................................................     ......................................................

......................................................     ......................................................

Complete the sentences with a verb + reflexive pronoun or *get* + past participle.

| | | | | | | | | |
|---|---|---|---|---|---|---|---|---|
| burn | enjoy | ~~attack~~ | scald | mug | bite | look after | | injure |
| introduce | run over | ~~weigh~~ | cut | | | | | |

Examples: I ..*weighed myself*.......... *on the bathroom scales.*
        They ..*got attacked*............ *the other night but luckily none of them was hurt badly.*

1. I ...................................................... by mosquitoes in the night.

2. He ...................................................... with that sharp knife when he was cooking.

3. She ...................................................... when she lit those candles.

4. They really ...................................................... at the party last night.

5. It was very dark and I ...................................................... coming through the tunnel.
   Fortunately I wasn't carrying much money on me at the time.

6. That poor little girl ...................................................... trying to cross the road. It
   wasn't really the driver's fault either.

7. There was nobody to help us when we arrived, so we had to ......................................................

8. She accidentally spilt some boiling water and ...................................................... .

9. He can't play because he ...................................................... last week. Somebody
   dropped a chair on his foot and it broke a small bone.

10. She ...................................................... but five minutes later I couldn't remember her name.

## 4 Odd one out

In each group of words, the underlined sound in one word is different from the others. Which one?

1. cr<u>ow</u>d   sh<u>ow</u>er   h<u>ow</u>ever   elb<u>ow</u>
2. h<u>ur</u>t   t<u>ur</u>n   h<u>u</u>rry   p<u>ur</u>pose
3. phr<u>a</u>se   f<u>a</u>vourite   p<u>a</u>tience   f<u>a</u>sten
4. s<u>u</u>ppose   p<u>u</u>blic   c<u>u</u>stomer   st<u>u</u>ck
5. q<u>ue</u>ue   <u>u</u>sed   s<u>u</u>permarket   m<u>u</u>sician

CD Listen to the recording to check your answers.

## 5 Another ordinary day

Read the story, then go back and make any changes you think are necessary for the story to be logical and comprehensible.

---

**8.40am**

*go out*

It was a miserable day but I decided to ~~stay in~~ and spend some money. I had breakfast and then went to my local bank. The cashier wasn't very cheerful but I cashed him a cheque and then I set off for town. On the way someone stopped me and said he was looking for the nearest bank. I told him I was a stranger, and he thanked me and walked off in the opposite direction.

It was now ten o'clock and the roads were getting quite quiet. I met an old friend who asked me for the money he owed me. I told him I was in a hurry and I walked off slowly to find a taxi.

I went into a coffee bar. It was almost full except for one table where a young couple were obviously having a very intimate conversation.

Later I found myself on a street corner next to an old lady. Suddenly, out of nowhere, a youth came running down the street, grabbed her bag and walked away. A man on the opposite side of the street saw nothing and shouted for help. I ran to the nearest phone box and rang the police. By now it was pouring with rain and I decided to go home. I saw a bus coming down the street, so I pushed my way to the back of the queue and got off.

When I got home I locked the front door and went in. I was feeling quite tired and I fell asleep on the sofa and got undressed.

---

Compare your story with the suggested answer in the Answer Key on page 143.

## 6 Guess what she's talking about

**A** What could someone be talking about here? Make two or three guesses, but don't look at the Answer Key.

Example: *You do this when you're getting dressed. You need two hands.*
   *do your buttons up, fasten a belt, put on your trousers*

1. You do this in a car, before you drive off.

   ..........................................................................................

2. You do this when you arrive at a hotel.

   ..........................................................................................

3. You do this in the garden or the house.

   ..........................................................................................

4. You do this when you have bought something for someone.

........................................................................................................................

5. You do this when you leave the house.

........................................................................................................................

6. This might happen to you when you are doing the washing up.

........................................................................................................................

**B** 🎧 Listen to the recording. Two people are playing a guessing game. What was the person thinking of in each case?

## 7 Please *do* something!

**A** Read the letter of complaint and decide what order the sentences should go in. Then decide which sentences should go together in paragraphs.

34 Kington Drive
Mornington
Warwickshire
January 18th

The Manager
Metro Bank
Mornington
Warwickshire

Dear Sir or Madam,

I have tried going to the bank at different times of the day; undoubtedly lunchtime is the worst time, but I never seem to get served without a wait of at least ten minutes.

I have now reached the point where I can no longer tolerate the queues in your branch.

This is common practice in most branches these days, so I am surprised that it is not used in your branch.

Firstly, the branch appears seriously understaffed relative to the number of customers.

I have had a current account with your bank for over twenty years, and have used your branch for the last two years, since I moved to Mornington.

I look forward to hearing from you on this matter.

I think there are two reasons for this.

And secondly, each counter position has a separate queue.

If this is the case, you clearly need to employ more people.

It would make much more sense to have a single queue, and for people to go to a counter as soon as one becomes free.

Yours faithfully,

Simon Jones

**B** Write your own letter about a queuing problem either at the ticket office of your local station or at a supermarket checkout, or any other queuing situation you have. Adapt the model letter above.

## 8 Speaking partners

**A** Can you think of any strange or amusing incidents that happened to you in any of these contexts? Tell your speaking partner about one or two of them.

Something that happened ...
- when you were having a bath or a shower.
- when you were getting dressed.
- when you were travelling somewhere, perhaps on holiday.
- when you were buying something recently.
- when you were having a walk, and minding your own business.
- when you were waiting for someone.
- when you were looking after someone else's child or pet.

Example: *A couple of weeks ago, I was staying at my uncle's house, and I was having a shower and suddenly the door bell rang. There was no one else in, so I got out of the shower and put a towel round me and opened the door. There was a little boy of about 6 there, and he started singing. He had a beautiful voice, but it was a bit embarrassing listening to him like that without my clothes on, so I gave him some money and sent him away.*

**B** Play the guessing game as in Exercise 6. Think of your own action, then give your partner a clue.

**C** Which are the most boring chores you have to do every day? Are there any daily chores which you find satisfying or enjoy doing?

## 9 Reflections

This space is for you to make a note of things you have learnt in this unit. You can also use it as a diary to write about your problems and progress in English.

....................................................................................................................................

....................................................................................................................................

....................................................................................................................................

....................................................................................................................................

....................................................................................................................................

....................................................................................................................................

....................................................................................................................................

....................................................................................................................................

....................................................................................................................................

....................................................................................................................................

....................................................................................................................................

....................................................................................................................................

....................................................................................................................................

....................................................................................................................................

....................................................................................................................................

Unit 6  LIFE'S LITTLE CHORES

# COURSES

## 1  I studied maths and chemistry

**Are the 's' endings in these sentences correct or not?**

1. She's studying physics and maths at university.
2. He is very keen on athletics and gymnastics but his sister hates physical exercises.
3. I attended two seminars on statistics but I gave it up because I couldn't understand it.
4. The economics problems in the country are almost impossible to solve.
5. She is training to be an electronics engineer.
6. I love going to arts galleries.
7. Studying foreign languages is one of my great pleasures in life.
8. Economics is a more difficult subject than electronics.
9. He's following the family tradition and is starting a course in medicines.
10. Politics is not a topic that interests me.

## 2  The person I most admire

Complete the third word in each sentence, using *who*, *that* or nothing. (More than one answer may be possible.)

1. The woman ........................ has helped me most in my life is ............................................... .

2. The thing ........................ I most enjoyed doing when I was a child was
..................................................................................... .

3. The season ........................ most people like best is ............................................. .

4. The people ........................ I'm closest to are ............................................... .

5. The thing ........................ would give me most satisfaction in life is
..................................................................................... .

6. The film ........................ most frightened me when I was a child was
..................................................................................... .

7. The man ........................ I most admire is ............................................... .

8. The possession ........................ I would save from a house fire would be
..................................................................................... .

Now complete the sentences using your own words. Compare with your speaking partner next time you see them.

Rewrite each of the dialogues in a reported form, using *ask* or *tell someone (not) to do something*.

Example: MAN: *Can I borrow a pen?*
WOMAN: *Yes, but give it back quickly!*
**He asked her to lend him a pen.**
**She told him to give it back quickly.**

1. A: Come with me, please.
   B: Could you wait a moment?

2. A: Can you put the TV on?
   B: Do it yourself!

4. A: Could you book a table for tonight?
   B: All right, but don't be late.

3. A: Move your car, please.
   B: OK, but please don't give me a ticket!

5. A: Please don't forget the shopping.
   B: Well, write me a list, then.

📖 Read this text silently and then listen to it on the recording. Notice how the voice rises and falls, and where it pauses.

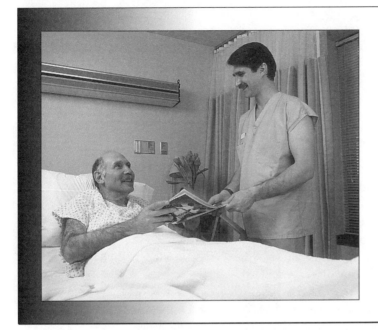

The thing that changed my life was when I <u>failed</u> my first year exams at university. I'd <u>enrolled on a course</u> in philosophy – I'll never really know why. I think it was what my father wanted me to do. Anyway, I knew when I sat the exam that I was going to fail quite spectacularly, and even before the <u>results</u> were out, I decided to change <u>career</u>. I realised I needed something more practical. And the next day, I walked into the university medical department and <u>applied</u> for a course in nursing. I've never <u>regretted</u> it.

Now listen to the same passage again. This time there are pauses for you to repeat part of a sentence after the speaker. If possible record yourself. How does your recording compare? What are the main differences?

**5 A turning point in my life**                                                                 writing

The text in Exercise 4 was about a turning point in someone's career choice. Here is a similar story about a turning point in someone's education.

The thing that changed my life was when I was still <u>at school</u>; I was 16, and I had no idea what I was going to do with my life. And my French <u>teacher</u> stopped me in the corridor one day and told me my homework was very good. I was quite pleased really, and then she went on to <u>suggest</u> that I went to university <u>to study</u> French. And I was so surprised I thought: 'Well, why not?' So I did, and I loved it. And here I am now living in France, married to a Frenchman and teaching English.

Now write a paragraph about a turning point in your education or career choice. Try to include at least three of the words underlined in this text or the one in Exercise 4. Begin your paragraph like this:

The thing that changed my life was …

📼 Listen to the recording and answer the questions. When you have finished, check with the tapescript on page 133.

Read the text and underline all the different courses. There are 16, and the first has been done for you.

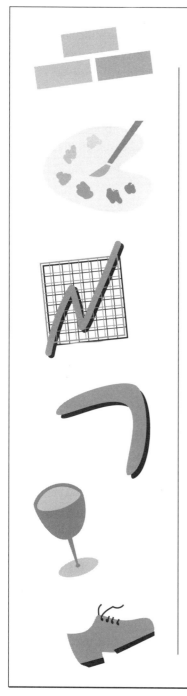

Weekend and holiday study courses have become very popular in Britain in the last few years, and there is an enormous range on offer. A booklet called *Time to Learn* provides information on what is available and makes fascinating reading on the state of the nation.

Take for example one weekend in April at the Old Rectory, near Pulborough in Sussex, where you can do a course in bricklaying, another in watercolour painting and a third in making your own stock market decisions.

Entry qualifications to weekend courses are generous, that is, generally no qualifications are necessary, apart from an ability to pay the fees, which may be quite high, as in the case of a one-month course in 'Ecology and technology' at Schumacher College in Devon.

'Beginners' is a common description of the kind of person welcome; 'complete beginners' can try glass engraving at West Dean College, Chichester, or 'Singing for the tone deaf' at Westham College near Warwick, or even 'Drawing and painting for the terrified' at Urchfont Manor College, Devizes.

Meanwhile, Ammerdown Centre near Bath provides instruction in walking in a sacred manner. Creative Holidays of Newlyn in Cornwall teaches, as well as cookery and shoemaking, a week of 'Zero balancing – body energy with body structure'.

Why do the holiday activities at Millfield School in Somerset include a course in karaoke singing? This art form is completely ruined if you do it well. A better proposition is 'Change your life' or, at Braziers Adult College in Oxfordshire, you can learn how to go about 'Living with more meaning'. That may help you with the 'Write your life story' course at Westham College. Here too is one of the most improbable courses taught outside Australia: boomerang flying.

No, I don't know if the students keep coming back.

Look at the words you underlined. Which are to do with:

– art?
– music?
– practical things you do with your hands?
– improving your mind?

## 8 Speaking partners

**A** Compare your answers to Exercise 2.

**B** What kind of weekend or holiday courses are there in your country? Have you ever done one, or do you know someone who has done one? Describe it. Which of the courses in Exercise 7 might interest you, and why?

**C** Choose any of the following statements to discuss with your speaking partner.

- Holidays and weekends are for relaxing and seeing family and friends, not for doing courses.
- The best way to learn any new skill or hobby is to do a course in it.
- Courses are a great way to make new friends.
- Nobody can teach you to change your life.
- If you choose to go on a course, you learn more than if someone (e.g. your company) makes you go.


## 9 Visual dictionary

Complete the visual dictionary for Unit 7 on page 120.


## 10 Reflections

This space is for you to make a note of things you have learnt in this unit. You can also use it as a diary to write about your problems and progress in English.

...................................................................................................................................
...................................................................................................................................
...................................................................................................................................
...................................................................................................................................
...................................................................................................................................
...................................................................................................................................
...................................................................................................................................
...................................................................................................................................
...................................................................................................................................
...................................................................................................................................
...................................................................................................................................
...................................................................................................................................
...................................................................................................................................
...................................................................................................................................
...................................................................................................................................

# ALL IN A DAY'S WORK

## 1  Do you think you could ...?                                    functional language

Find the four mistakes in each of these dialogues. Then check your answers in the
Answer Key on page 144.

A: Hello?
B: Is that Damien Lewis?
A: Speaking.
B: Here is Carol Robins, Mr Lewis.
A: Hello, Carol, how can I help you?
B: Well, I very much like to come and see you this week.
A: I'm afraid that's impossible. You see, I'm going away tomorrow for a few days.
B: OK, well, perhaps I can make an appointment with you for next week then?
A: Fine. How about Tuesday at 10.00?
B: I'm very sorry but I'm occupied myself at 10.00. Would it be all right that I come at 11.00?
A: That's fine. I'd be grateful if you could tell my secretary.
B: Sure. Many thanks.

A: (*Opening the front door*) Hello, Harry. Come in!
B: Thanks, Colin. Look, er, I wonder if you could borrow your ladder. We've got a problem
   with the roof and …
A: Oh, I'm afraid but that's a bit difficult. Well, in fact, impossible. Someone has stolen it.
B: Oh, no. I am sorry.
A: Actually, would it be possible that you take me to the police station to report it? My car's
   broken down.
B: Of course. Do you mind that I stop at the post office on the way?
A: No, that's fine.
B: Right. Let's go, then.

## 2  It's in black and white                              vocabulary: fixed phrases

On page 56 of the Class Book you saw a number of phrases in which two words are
joined by *and*. The order of words is fixed:

Examples:  *pros and cons* (not *cons and pros*)
           *for and against* (not *against and for*)

Choose pairs of words from the box that go together, and then complete the sentences
below with the words in the right order. A good monolingual dictionary will help you
because if you look up one of the words, the dictionary should give you the phrase.

| black | demand | advantages | tidy | Mr | neat | disadvantages |
| wrong | ups | supply | profit | loss | Mrs | white | right | downs |

1. You must address the letter to ............................. and ............................. Thompson.

2. The boss doesn't wear a suit every day, but she always looks very ............................. and

   ............................. .

3. There are obviously ............................. and ............................. to this new plan, so we

   must look at it very carefully.

4. We've got the books and they need them, so it's a simple matter of .......................... and
   .......................... .

5. If you want that financial information, you will need to look at the ..........................
   and .......................... figures for the last three years.

6. The company has had its .......................... and .......................... over the years, but
   now things are quite stable, I believe.

7. Read the contract – it's all there in .......................... and .......................... .

8. The way some people behave makes you think they don't know the difference between
   .......................... and .......................... .


## 3 Pros and cons, good and bad

work vocabulary

Complete these questions with a suitable opposite.

Example: *Do you think you are flexible or* .inflexible............... ?
         *Did you win the contract or* .lose it............. ?

1. Do you prefer to give orders or ..............................................?

2. Is that company making a loss or ..............................................?

3. Are your holidays paid or ..............................................?

4. Do you keep your problems to yourself or ..............................................?

5. Are you self-employed or do you ..............................................?

6. Do you lack security in your job or ..............................................?

7. Are you for this idea or ..............................................?

8. Do you agree with me or ..............................................?

9. Is that an advantage or ..............................................?

10. Did you avoid a decision or ..............................................?

## 4 Putting it nicely

permission and requests

Rewrite these sentences in a more polite and diplomatic way. Try not to use the same phrase more than twice.

Examples: *Give me those books.*
**Do you think you could give me those books?**
*They can't leave the office until five o'clock.*
**I'm afraid they can't leave the office until five o'clock.**

1. OK if I take the afternoon off?

.......................................................................................................

2. You can't go on that training course.

.......................................................................................................

3. Shut the door on your way out.

.......................................................................................................

4. You can't leave early this afternoon.

.......................................................................................................

5. Take this to the accounts office.

.......................................................................................................

6. Send me the documents as soon as possible.

.......................................................................................................

7. It's cold in here. I'm going to close the window.

.......................................................................................................

8. Lend me £5.

.......................................................................................................

## 5 Listen and answer

work vocabulary; listening

 Listen to the recording and write down your answers.

## 6 What's good about it?

reading

Read this paragraph and instruction. When you have finished, read the list on page 44 written by an American. Tick (✓) any which you wrote down yourself, and underline any which are also true for you.

MOST PEOPLE, when they have a serious disappointment or disaster, go through stages of ignoring the problem, then anger, then depression. These stages paralyse their thinking. Sidney X Shore has invented a simple but very effective method of finding a way out of this difficult period. It consists of writing out all the things that are *good* about a difficult situation. People begin to see the situation in a new light. They may develop new attitudes to the problem.
Would you like to try it? If so, read on.

Take five minutes. List all the possible thoughts and ideas about this question:

**What's *good* about losing your job from tomorrow?**

EXAMPLES:

*I now have time to stop and think what I really want to do in life.*

*My boss was impossible: I'm happy to be away from him/her.*

Now you continue.

**A** Look at the situations on page 55 in the Class Book again. Read the two memos below and answer these questions.

1. Which situation on page 55 do the memos relate to?
2. Which memo do you think Alex should send, and why?
3. What language in the memos was used in the lesson in the Class Book?

**MEMO**

**From:** Alex Robinson

**To:** Joan Conrad

**Date:** 15th April

Further to our meeting last week, I think there are a few things we still need to talk about. I realise you are very busy at the moment, but would it be possible for you to meet me again briefly one afternoon next week? I'll ring you tomorrow to see if we can fix a time together.

**MEMO**

**From:** Alex Robinson

**To:** Joan Conrad

**Date:** 15th April

After last week's meeting, it's clear we still have a lot to discuss and agree on. Would it be all right if I came over to your office next Tuesday after lunch – say at 2.30?

**B** Now write one of the following.

Situation 1
You want to attend a weekend conference relating to your work and you are hoping that your company will pay for the cost of the conference and your accommodation. Your boss asks you to put your request in writing, giving your reasons for wanting to go.

Situation 2
You need a day off because you are moving into a new flat. Your boss is in a meeting all day, but the boss's secretary has agreed to pass him/her a memo from you during a break. Write a short memo to make your request. Remember, the department is particularly busy at the moment.

**8 Speaking partners**

**A** Make sure you have both done Exercise 6 in this unit of the Personal Study Workbook. If not, do it together now.

Choose another disaster situation, like losing your job, and together make a list of what is good about it. Think of your own disaster or choose from one of these:

– What's good about losing your address book?
– What's good about your car being stolen?
– What's good about going to prison for a week?

**B** Are you a 'manager' in a work situation, or in your own home? For example, are you a parent who has to manage a family? Do you manage anything in a social situation, like a club or a team?

If so, tell your speaking partner about the situation. What do you like about being a manager, and what don't you like?

## WHAT'S GOOD ABOUT LOSING YOUR JOB FROM TOMORROW?

● I've lasted longer in this job than anyone ever expected.

● I've gotten* experience which will be helpful in a new job.

● I really wanted to get a different job anyway.

● I can land a new job that pays me at least 25% more.

● I can now move to Arizona (Florida, California) where I've always wanted to live.

● I'll now have time for a much-needed vacation.

● I've discovered new strengths in myself in dealing with crises, and I feel good about that.

● My relatives are standing by me with aid and comfort, which I never expected.

● My severance pay, together with my new job will put me ahead financially.

● I begin to know who my true friends are.

● I can find a more interesting job, suited to my abilities.

● I can now go into business on my own – something I've always wanted.

● My partner can now have a career of his/her own.

● I have the time to work on decorating the house.

● I can now do more sports and hobbies.

*gotten = American English*
*got = British English*

---

## 9 Reflections

This space is for you to make a note of things you have learnt in this unit. You can also use it as a diary to write about your problems and progress in English.

...............................................................................................................................
...............................................................................................................................
...............................................................................................................................
...............................................................................................................................
...............................................................................................................................
...............................................................................................................................
...............................................................................................................................
...............................................................................................................................
...............................................................................................................................
...............................................................................................................................
...............................................................................................................................
...............................................................................................................................
...............................................................................................................................
...............................................................................................................................
...............................................................................................................................

# FROM THE CRADLE TO THE GRAVE

## 1 Sentence transformations

passives

Change these sentences into the present simple passive (*is/are* + past participle) or the past simple passive (*was/were* + past participle).

1. Friends give money to the bride and groom.

   The bride and groom ..........................................................................................

2. They export the cars to Europe.

   ..........................................................................................................................

3. They took the man to hospital.

   ..........................................................................................................................

4. I sent the books last week.

   ..........................................................................................................................

5. They perform the play every year.

   ..........................................................................................................................

6. Kurosawa directed the film.

   ..........................................................................................................................

7. Police arrested the man outside the theatre.

   ..........................................................................................................................

8. They make these sweets in Turkey.

   ..........................................................................................................................

## 2 Countries and nationalities

vocabulary

**A** In the word puzzle there are fourteen important cities (vertically or horizontally). Find them and then write down the country each one is in.

```
B P O C S C H O I
U R V A T H E N S
C A I R O E R A T
H G E A C L I M A
A U N C K S Y O N
R E N A H I A S B
E R A S O N D L U
S E O U L K H O L
T R A N M I L A N
```

**B** Now write down the nationality of the people from each of the countries.

Example: *Italy*   **Italian**

## 3 Birth, marriage and death

Complete these sentences with the correct word.

1. At the wedding the ........................, whose name was Maria, wore a cream-coloured
   dress, and the ........................ wore a dark grey suit.
2. The wedding ........................ lasted about half an hour, and was conducted by a
   Catholic ........................ who knew Maria's parents very well.
3. After the wedding the newly-married couple went to Greece for their ........................ .
4. Three years later their first baby was ........................ . It was a boy and it was
   ........................ in the local church.
5. And two years after the ........................ of their first child, Maria became
   ........................ again. This time she hoped it would be a girl. It was.
6. A year later Maria's grandmother died, and they held the ........................ service in the
   same church where Maria got married.
7. After the service Maria's grandmother was ........................ in the churchyard next to
   her husband who had died five years earlier.
8. In her ........................ she left all her money and possessions to Maria's young children.

## 4 You are obliged to

Correct any mistakes of grammar or fact in these sentences.

1. When you enter a foreign country, you are not usually obliged to show a passport or other
   form of identification.
2. You haven't to wear a crash helmet in a car.
3. You aren't allowed use someone else's passport as if it was yours.
4. In certain countries in the world, women aren't supposed to leave their arms or legs
   uncovered.
5. In some Arab countries, you cannot bought or consume alcohol.
6. In most countries, parents obliged to educate their children.
7. If you travel to certain parts of the world, you are supposed to take fresh food through
   customs without declaring it.
8. In most countries, you must to have a licence if you own a gun.

## 5 Same or different?

Look at the underlined letters in each of the pairs of words. Is the pronunciation the
same or different?

Examples: cradle and grave (same)
          stage and stand (different)

1. bride and bridge
2. ceremony and cremation
3. groom and food
4. religion and decision
5. burial and custom
6. veil and receive
7. funeral and future
8. allow and throw

▭▭ Listen to the recording and check your answers.

Read the list of minimum ages for English and Welsh law, using a dictionary if necessary. Make a note of any new words that you learn.

Do any of the laws surprise you? Underline them. Next time you see your speaking partner, discuss them together.

| AGE | |
|---|---|
| at birth | A bank account can be opened in the child's name. |
| 6 weeks | The child can be given to prospective adopters. |
| 3 years | The child must be paid for on public transport. |
| 5 years | The child is obliged to receive full-time education, and is allowed to drink alcohol in private. |
| 10 years | The child can be convicted of a crime if it can be shown that he/she knew it was wrong. |
| 12 years | The child is allowed to buy a pet. |
| 13 years | The child can open a current bank account, at the discretion of the manager. |
| 14 years | The child can:<br>take a part-time job.<br>be convicted of a criminal offence as if they were an adult (although the trial and sentence will be different).<br>own an airgun.<br>go into a bar with an adult, but is not allowed to buy or consume alcoholic drink. |
| 15 years | The child can own a shot gun and ammunition. |
| 16 years | The child can:<br>get married with parental consent.<br>consent to medical treatment and choose their own doctor.<br>leave school and work full time.<br>join a trade union.<br>drive a moped or tractor.<br>fly solo in a glider.<br>buy cigarettes. (He/she can smoke at any age.)<br>The child is:<br>obliged to pay full fare on public transport.<br>entitled to join the armed forces with parental consent. |
| 17 years | The child can:<br>drive a car or motor cycle.<br>fly a plane solo.<br>be tried on any charge in an adult court, and be sent to prison. |
| 18 years | The child becomes an adult and can:<br>vote.<br>marry without parental consent.<br>change his/her name.<br>apply for a passport.<br>own land (including a house).<br>do jury service.<br>make a will.<br>be tattooed.<br>be admitted to see a film with an '18' certificate.<br>join the armed services without parental consent. |
| 21 years | The adult can now:<br>stand in a general or local election.<br>drive a lorry or bus. |

## 7 Melinda's wedding

📖 Listen to the woman on the recording talking about her wedding and decide if these statements are true or false.

 1. She and her husband got married in church.
 2. They wrote a guest list and a list of food needed.
 3. She made her dress herself.
 4. Her husband hired a suit and top hat.
 5. A friend who was an opera singer sang during the ceremony.
 6. The bridesmaid forgot her flowers.
 7. The service was beautiful and people cried.
 8. They drank champagne and people made speeches.
 9. After cutting the wedding cake, they went to the pub.
10. They had a two-week honeymoon in the sun.

## 8 Sorry, we've changed our minds!

It is not uncommon for the couple getting married to change their minds and decide not to get married after all. Of course, if a lot of arrangements have been made, or presents have been received, it is a little embarrassing. However, if the couple cancel the wedding, presents they have given each other in anticipation of the wedding should be returned – including any engagement ring. And of course, any presents sent by friends or relatives are normally returned.

So the couple may have to write any of these letters:

– to the church or registry office to cancel the arrangements
– to the hotel, restaurant, etc. who will need to cancel the booking
– to anyone who has sent presents, returning the gifts and explaining what has happened
– to anyone invited to the ceremony/reception

According to etiquette, these letters are written by the bride's mother. She usually thanks people for what they have done or given, and expresses regret.

Read this letter, and then write one of your own to one of the more official bodies or to a guest who has sent a present.

> 15 Leamington Villas,
> Boston,
> Lincolnshire.
>
> May 21st 1996
>
> Dear Mr and Mrs Barrington,
>
> I am very sorry to have to tell you that the John and Maureen's wedding on the 6th of July has been cancelled. They have decided not to go ahead with it for personal reasons, and although we are all very sad about it, they feel it is for the best.
>
> It is a great pity that we will not be seeing you after all, but let's hope that we will be able to meet later in the year.
>
> With very best wishes,
>
> Madeleine Bright

## 9 Speaking partners

**A** Look at the minimum ages in Exercise 6. Discuss any that are different from your own country.

**B** What was the last wedding ceremony you went to? Whose was it, and what happened?

**C** Are there any wedding or funeral customs in your country that have changed in your lifetime?

## 10 Visual dictionary

Complete the visual dictionary for Unit 9 on page 121.

## 11 Reflections

This space is for you to make a note of things you have learnt in this unit. You can also use it as a diary to write about your problems and progress in English.

.................................................................................................................
.................................................................................................................
.................................................................................................................
.................................................................................................................
.................................................................................................................
.................................................................................................................
.................................................................................................................
.................................................................................................................
.................................................................................................................
.................................................................................................................
.................................................................................................................
.................................................................................................................
.................................................................................................................
.................................................................................................................
.................................................................................................................

# PHONAHOLICS

**A  Complete these phone conversations in a suitable way.**

1. A: Hello?

   B: Oh, hello. ................................. Maria?

   A: No, it's Ursula. I'm afraid Maria's ................................. .

   B: Oh, right. Do you know what time ................................. ?

   A: Uh, later this afternoon, I think – about five o'clock.

   B: I see. Well, in that case, could I ................................. ?

   A: Yes, of course. ................................. , I'll just ................... a pen. OK, go ahead.

   B: Right. Could you ask her to ring me when she ................................. ? My
      name is Catherine. She's got my number.

   A: OK, ................................. as soon as she gets in.

   B: Thanks very much. Bye.

   A: Bye.

2. A: Morton and Benson, Solicitors. Can I help you?

   B: Yes, ................................. Catherine Benson, please?

   A: Yes, ................................. ?

   B: My name is Derek Silver. I'm an old client of hers.

   A: Right, Mr Silver. If you'd just like to hold the line for a moment,

      ................................. .

   B: OK, thanks.

3. A: Hello.

   B: Hi, Sarah, ................................. James. How are you?

   A: ................................. . And you?

   B: Yeah, I'm OK. Listen I'm ................................. about this evening. I need to
      ask you a big ................................. .

   A: Oh, yes. What is it?

   B: Well, I'm afraid I've got no transport. Do you think you could
      ................................. to the party in your car?

   A: Yeah, sure, of course.

   B: Oh, great. Thanks a lot.

   A: What time ................................. pick you up, then?

   B: Eight?

   A: Yes, that's fine. I'll ................................. .

   B: Yes, OK. Bye.

**B**  🎧  **Now listen to the answers on the recording and compare them with your own.**

Cities and countries sometimes change their names.

Example:  *Tunis used to be Carthage.*
          *Bangladesh used to be part of Pakistan.*

Write similar sentences, combining place names from the two boxes.

| |
|---|
| ~~Tunis~~    ~~Bangladesh~~    Zaire    Thailand    St Petersburg    Slovakia |
| Ghana    Estonia    Iran    Istanbul    Sri Lanka    Zimbabwe |

| |
|---|
| ~~Carthage~~    ~~Pakistan~~    Rhodesia    Leningrad    Ceylon    The Gold Coast |
| Siam    the USSR    Constantinople    Czechoslovakia    Belgian Congo |
| Persia |

---

**3 Cheque book and bookshop**              vocabulary: compounds and collocation

Put a word in the brackets that will form a compound word or phrase with the word
before and the word after.

The missing words you need are all in the box below.

Example:  cheque ( *book* ) shop

1. answer (..........................) number

2. burglar (..........................) call

3. telephone (..........................) enquiries

4. fax (..........................) gun

5. phone (..........................) office

6. marketing (..........................) store

7. extension (..........................) plate

8. lunch (..........................) table

9. physical (..........................) book

| |
|---|
| alarm    directory    machine    exercise    time    box    department |
| number    phone    ~~book~~ |

---

## 4 Harmless inventions

Put these twelve words from Unit 10 into the correct columns, *adjective* or *verb*, below.

> hostile    invent    refuse    aggressive    safe    destroy    violent
> harmless    install    accept    friendly    deteriorate

| Adjective | Noun | Verb | Noun |
|---|---|---|---|
| .................... | .................... | .................... | .................... |
| .................... | .................... | .................... | .................... |
| .................... | .................... | .................... | .................... |
| .................... | .................... | .................... | .................... |
| .................... | .................... | .................... | .................... |
| .................... | .................... | .................... | .................... |

Now complete the *noun* column for all twelve words.

## 5 Making excuses on the phone

Read the text and fill the gaps with these phrases.

> just stepped out of the room    in a meeting    Go away
> doesn't want to speak to you    at his desk    going to be tied up all day
> wants to speak to you    still at lunch

When you try to ring someone 'important', you often get through to their secretary who says, 'I'll just see if he's [1]................................ ...................................' This suggests the incredible idea that an assistant can't actually see the boss without going on a small expedition. The real meaning is, 'I'll just ask him if he [2]...................................' Often the secretary will achieve the same end by asking, 'And what did you say your name was?' and then repeating your name (as if writing it down) in a voice loud enough for the boss to hear and make a decision.

Another strategy is to say, 'He's not at his desk right now' and 'He's [3]................................ ...................................,' 'He's taken a late lunch' also comes into this category, because its real purpose is to protect the boss. The real meaning is: 'Even though it's five o'clock, he's [4]...................... and may well be drunk.' Offering very little hope of speaking to the boss is, 'I'm afraid

he's [5]................................ ...................................' This very rarely means that the person is actually in a meeting. It usually means, 'He [6]....................................' Still more dismissive is, 'I'm afraid he's tied up at the moment', or even worse, 'I'm sorry, he's [7]......................, ...................' Sometimes this is used in a horrible rejection like, 'I'm sorry, he's not at his desk right now, but I know he's going into an outside conference soon, and then he'll be tied up for the rest of the day ...' and 'I've no idea when he'll be free.' This, loosely translated, means '[8]................ ....................,'

RUDE NOISES ON THE PHONE

**A** 📖 You will hear one half of a phone conversation (in other words, only one of the two speakers). What is the relationship between the speakers, and what is the reason for the call?

**B** Write down four answers you think the other speaker gave.

---

**7 Don't forget to call the office** writing: messages

**A** Read these situations and look at the messages the people left.

1. James is staying at his friend Marta's house. While she is out, the vet telephones to say that Marta's dog, which she took to the vet yesterday, is now much better. He suggests that someone should collect the dog that afternoon.

Marta
The vet rang. The dog is better.
You can collect him this
afternoon.
          James

2. Peter Maxwell is expecting to meet an Australian client (Mrs Beresford) in her hotel in his home town. He gets to the hotel and waits for an hour but she doesn't arrive. He has an important appointment with another client in another part of town, so he writes a message to explain the problem and suggest another meeting.

THE SWAN HOTEL
*Petersford*

Mrs Beresford
I waited until 3 and then I had to go to
another meeting. Sorry. I'll ring you this evening
to fix another appointment.
                    Peter Maxwell

**B** Now write suitable messages for these situations.

1. While you are at work, you receive an urgent telephone call from home asking you to come home quickly. Your assistant, Peter, is out at lunch. Leave a message for him, explain what has happened and ask him to cancel your afternoon appointments.
2. While you are staying at your friend Simon's house, Simon's sister rings. Simon is out, and his sister explains to you that she would like Simon to ring her back before she leaves the office at 6.00.
3. Someone telephones you at home and wants to speak to your brother, Paul, who is a student. He is very angry that your brother did not return the books that he borrowed to write his essay. The caller (Max) urgently needs the books for his own essay by this evening.

## 8 Speaking partners

**A** Think of a place you are both in now where you could ring for information *in English*.

Examples: *an English-speaking airline company*
*a large hotel*
*a British, American or Australian shop*
*an embassy*

With your partner, agree in advance on the information you want.

Example: *Airline company: you want to know the times, prices and availability of flights to a particular destination.*

Both of you separately make your calls *in English*, and then compare the information you receive.

**B** Can you think of any interesting, strange or amusing things that have happened to you recently while using the telephone? Tell your partner.

## 9 Reflections

This space is for you to make a note of things you have learnt in this unit. You can also use it as a diary to write about your problems and progress in English.

..............................................................................................................................................................
..............................................................................................................................................................
..............................................................................................................................................................
..............................................................................................................................................................
..............................................................................................................................................................
..............................................................................................................................................................
..............................................................................................................................................................
..............................................................................................................................................................
..............................................................................................................................................................
..............................................................................................................................................................
..............................................................................................................................................................
..............................................................................................................................................................
..............................................................................................................................................................
..............................................................................................................................................................
..............................................................................................................................................................

# GOODS AND SERVICES

---

## 1 If you don't keep the receipt ...

*if* sentences with *will, may* or *might*

**A** Match the sentence halves.

1. If you don't keep the receipt,
2. If you leave your shopping there,
3. If you don't have your windows cleaned soon,
4. If you ask the shop to gift-wrap the goods,
5. If you want to have some trousers shortened,
6. If you don't have your eyes tested,
7. If you use an electronic dictionary,
8. If you offer less than the asking price,

a. they might be offended.
b. they may let you choose the paper.
c. you might not realise your sight is getting worse.
d. you won't be able to see out.
e. someone might steal it.
f. you'll have to find a good tailor.
g. you'll be able to look things up quicker.
h. the shop might not give you a refund.

**B** Now think of a different ending for each of the sentences 1–8.

Example: *If you don't keep the receipt,* **you might be sorry later.**

---

## 2 Words ending *-able* or *-ible*

vocabulary: suffixes

**A** Which adjective is being defined in these sentences? The first five are quite easy but the second five are more difficult.

1. You can wash it.               It's ...................................................
2. You can break it.              It's ...................................................
3. You can inflate it.            It's ...................................................
4. You can adjust it.             It's ...................................................
5. You can't rely on it.          It's ...................................................
6. You can throw it away.         It's ...................................................
7. You can eat it.                It's ...................................................
8. You can carry it.              It's ...................................................
9. You can wear it inside out.    It's ...................................................
10. You can't read it because     It's ...................................................
    the handwriting is so bad.

**B** What could *it* be in each of the above sentences?

Example: *Sentence 1 could be a jumper or jacket.*

---

Choose a feature (or features) from the box for each of these products.

| no additives | showerproof | non-stick | low alcohol | extra strong |
| low calorie | dry clean only | free-range | shock-resistant | |

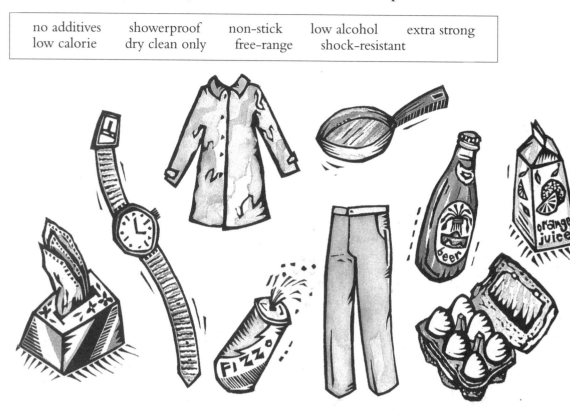

**4 Getting things done**                          pronunciation: sentence stress

**A** ⊡ Read the first conversation, and listen to the recording. The words in capitals are more prominent or stressed.

A: Have you had your HAIR cut?
B: Yes, I HAVE. In fact, I HAD it done this MORNING.
A: Well, it looks very NICE.
B: THANK you.

Practise saying the dialogue with the recording, stressing the words in capitals.

**B** The prominent words in these dialogues are missing. Complete the dialogues with a suitable word. Write it in capitals, as in the dialogue above.

C: Where did you have the ..*FILM*.. developed?

D: Oh, I sent it to a ............................. .

C: Were the photos ............................?

D: Mmm, they were ............................. .

E: Where are you ............................?

F: I'm going to have my ............................. tested.

E: Why? Do you need ............................?

F: I ............................. not!

G: Oh, no, my ............................. is broken.

H: Well, you'd better have it ............................. .

G: Yes, but ............................?

H: At a ............................., I suppose.

I: My ............................. has broken down again.

J: Oh, dear. What ............................?

I: I forgot to have it ............................. .

J: Well, that was ............................., wasn't it?

**C** ⊡ Listen to the recording and see if your stressed words are the same. Then practise saying your conversations and the ones on the recording.

Read the text and answer the questions.

# PURCHASING GOODS

When you buy something from a shop, you are protected by The Sale of Goods Act 1979, which lays down that the shopkeeper makes certain promises to the customer:

1. **The goods are fit for their usual use**
2. **The goods are of proper quality**
3. **The goods are as described**
4. **His sales talk is true**

### Promise No.1:    THE GOODS ARE FIT FOR THEIR USUAL USE

This means that you must be able to use the thing you buy for its normal use. For instance, if you buy a cake, it must be good enough to eat. Likewise, children's toys must be safe for children to play with.

### Promise No.2:    THE GOODS ARE OF PROPER QUALITY

It is not always easy to decide if goods are of proper quality. You have to ask yourself the question 'Should these goods have been sold in this condition?' And the key factors here are often the price of the goods and the way they were described. So, if you buy goods in a sale at a lower price, you can expect (and perhaps should expect) a lower standard.

However, examples of goods which are not of proper quality would be a clock that keeps poor time, or clothes that are torn, or cups and saucers that are cracked.

One difficult question is, 'How long can one expect an article to last before faults develop in it?' This will depend on the facts of the individual case, but, as always, the price and the description are very important. A watch costing £100 should last for several years without developing a fault, whereas a £5 watch cannot be expected to last as long.

### Promise No.3:    THE GOODS ARE AS DESCRIBED

Goods must be what they say they are. A 'salmon steak' must be made of salmon; a 100% wool pullover must not contain any other fibre than wool.

Related to the accuracy of the description of the goods is the accuracy of the 'sales talk'. This is the fourth promise.

### Promise No.4:    HIS SALES TALK IS TRUE

Salesmen can exaggerate a little about the goods they are selling. For example, it is acceptable to claim that a car is 'wonderful'; but they must not say anything which is factually incorrect. For example, a salesman cannot say that a car does 15 kilometres a litre, if in fact it only does 12 kilometres a litre.

Read through the following situations. Which of the above promises (1, 2, 3 or 4) are being broken?

1. You order a light-blue coat. When it arrives, it is dark blue.
2. You buy a shirt. When you get home, you discover that a button is missing.
3. You buy a raincoat and wear it the next day. There is a light shower of rain, and when you get home, the inside of the raincoat is wet.
4. You buy a book, but the print is so small that it is difficult to read. (You have normal eyesight and don't need glasses.)
5. When you buy a car, you are told that it is a 1994 model. From the documents you later discover that it is a 1993 model.
6. You buy an expensive pair of shoes and after one month the heel falls off.

**A** 📼 There are different ways of displaying goods inside a shop, and each one will have its special features. Listen and complete the table.

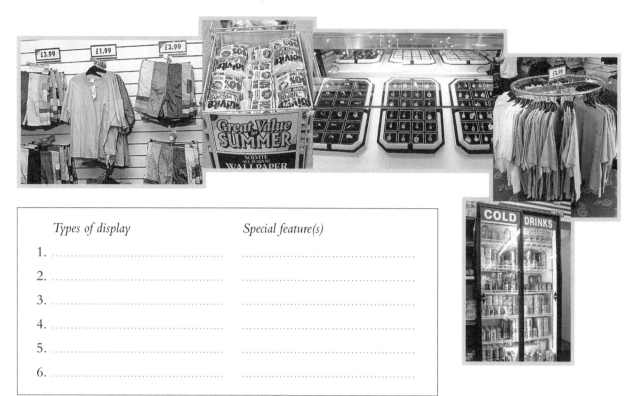

| Types of display | Special feature(s) |
|---|---|
| 1. ............................... | ............................... |
| 2. ............................... | ............................... |
| 3. ............................... | ............................... |
| 4. ............................... | ............................... |
| 5. ............................... | ............................... |
| 6. ............................... | ............................... |

**B** Can you think of two products that would be suitable for each type of display above?

---

**7 A letter of complaint**                                           writing: capital letters and spelling

**A** There are 7 spelling mistakes and 18 mistakes with capital letters in the text. Correct them.

```
                              14 wimpole street
                              london WC1
                              20 january, 1996

    dear mr robertson,

    last wenesday i recieved a pair of robertson's
    reversable trousers from your company by mail order.

    the parcel was damaged on arrival and the trousers
    were torn. they where also not the coulour i ordered.

    i would be greatful if you could replace them with a
    blue/grey pair, and refund the postage.

    yours sincerly,
    jack ellis
```

**B** If you wish, write your own letter of complaint about one of the products on page 77 of the Class Book.

## 8 Speaking partners

**A** Advertisements must be truthful, honest and decent. That means they must not tell lies about their product; they must not make false claims (for example, 'Drink this juice and you will have eternal youth'); and they must be decent (for example, not show naked people or have pictures which offend people).

With your speaking partner find some magazine advertisements, in English if possible, and discuss whether you think they are honest and truthful.

**B** If you are from different countries, tell your partner:

a. What different forms of shopping there are, and which are the most popular;
b. What the service is like in shops and the quality of after-sales service.

If you are from the same country, tell your partner:

a. What you think of your local shopping facilities;
b. What you think of service in different shops;
c. What shops are like in different towns and cities in your country.

## 9 Visual dictionary

Complete the visual dictionary for Unit 11 on page 122.

## 10 Reflections

This space is for you to make a note of things you have learnt in this unit. You can also use it as a diary to write about your problems and progress in English.

..................................................................................................................................................

..................................................................................................................................................

..................................................................................................................................................

..................................................................................................................................................

..................................................................................................................................................

..................................................................................................................................................

..................................................................................................................................................

..................................................................................................................................................

..................................................................................................................................................

..................................................................................................................................................

..................................................................................................................................................

..................................................................................................................................................

..................................................................................................................................................

..................................................................................................................................................

# BARE NECESSITIES

## 1 Frequency and degree adverbs

Choose the correct adverb(s) to complete each sentence. There may be more than one correct answer.

1. I thought the book was ................................... fantastic.

   a. very     b. extremely     c. absolutely

2. We used to love the cinema but we ................................... go now.

   a. rarely     b. regularly     c. hardly ever

3. She was ................................... exhausted by the end of the walk.

   a. absolutely     b. completely     c. very

4. I clean my room ................................... .

   a. regularly     b. hardly ever     c. never

5. It's ................................... time to go home.

   a. quite     b. nearly     c. almost

6. They told me it was ................................... interesting.

   a. absolutely     b. very     c. really

7. ................................... I walk to work.

   a. Occasionally     b. Always     c. Sometimes

8. I ................................... see my friends these days because I'm so busy at work.

   a. regularly     b. often     c. rarely

9. The food in that restaurant is ................................... good.

   a. extremely     b. absolutely     c. very

10. We don't visit them ...................................; just on special occasions.

    a. rarely     b. occasionally     c. regularly

## 2 Absolutely adjectives

Complete these sentences with a suitable adjective.

1. The water was absolutely ................................... .

2. He's a very good cook and the meal was absolutely ................................... .

3. My father was absolutely ................................... when I took his car without permission.

4. I thought her story was absolutely ................................... . I'm sure it can't be true.

5. The information about the trains is absolutely ..................................., otherwise we won't know when to leave.

6. The others loved the play but I thought it was absolutely ............................. .

7. I'm going to buy another can opener because this one is absolutely

   ............................. .

8. The house is quite big and the garden is absolutely ............................. . It has a
   swimming pool, a tennis court and hundreds of trees.

9. You must try that new restaurant. The food is absolutely ............................. .

10. I haven't got room for anything in my new flat; it's absolutely ............................. .

## 3 Dental floss and dental surgeon vocabulary: compounds

Find one word that could be used to form a compound with each of the words after it.
Sometimes a compound is written as one word, sometimes with a hyphen, and
sometimes as two words. Use a dictionary to help you.

Example:          *floss*

   _dental_ .........................

                  *surgeon*

1. .........................   plug        5. .........................   shade
                              ache                                    post

2. .........................   bag         6. .........................   room
                              pill                                    tyre

3. .........................   file        7. .........................   pick
                              varnish                                  ache

4. .........................   cut         8. .........................   horn
                              drier                                   lace

## 4 My heart beats noun + verb or verb + noun collocation

Complete these sentences with a logical verb.

1. The human heart ............................. around 70 times a minute.

2. Water starts to ............................. at 100 degrees centigrade.

3. The plane ............................. safely and the passengers got ready to leave.

4. Ice ............................. when the temperature starts to rise.

5. Some candles seem to ............................. quite quickly, while others last for ages.

6. I must ............................. the rubbish in my spare room because my cousin is coming
   to stay for a while.

7. The teacher asked us to ............................. places and work with a different partner.

8. I never ............................. a lot of money in the house.

9. If the water is cold, just ............................. it until it almost reaches boiling point.

10. We ............................. the room and it was about 6 metres by 4 metres.

The text below is about the things that American women carry in their handbags (called a *purse* in American English), and it includes a number of different words that mean *strange*. As you read underline all the examples you can find.

# WACKY THINGS THAT GIRLS CARRY AROUND WITH THEM

Women carry some of the oddest things in their purses – including such items as a baby tooth and a big rubber toe.

Lady shoppers at a large Florida shopping mall opened their handbags for a fun survey, and some of the things inside were downright wacky. The weirdest item, the big toe from a dog's rubber toy, belonged to Lynda Wylburn.

'I had to have my dog put to sleep last year and I've been carrying the toe from his rubber toy ever since,' said Lynda. 'It's something to remember him by.'

Nail technician Sue Moore packed something unusual inside her big purse – another purse. 'All the stuff I really need is inside the smaller purse,' said Sue. 'If I don't want to carry the big purse, I just pull out the small one.'

A screwdriver and a jar of Deep Heat (medication for stiff muscles) spilled out of Becky Schmid's bag, while inside Shirley Amendola's bag there was a tire* gauge, a shaving razor and one of her baby teeth. 'I planned to put the tooth in my safe-deposit box at the bank a few years ago,' said the 30-year-old medical assistant. 'It's a childhood memento. I never made it to the bank that day and the tooth has been in my purse ever since.'

Proud grandmother Phyllis Hale pulled out a piece of paper bearing her granddaughter's handprint. 'I've been meaning to get it framed,' said the 49-year-old office manager.

An electronic Spanish language interpreter was inside Phyllis Moloney's handbag. 'I got it for Christmas last year and it's been in my purse ever since. I just think it's handy to have it there in case I need to understand Spanish.'

* *tire* is spelt *tyre* in British English.

Based on the text, things may be in women's bags for different reasons. Complete this list.

1. *There are things that women put in their bags and then forget to take out e.g. the tooth.*

2. .....................................................................................................................

3. .....................................................................................................................

4. .....................................................................................................................

📼 Three people are describing a difficult situation they have been in. Listen and complete the table.

|  | Where did it happen? | What was the problem? | How long did it last? | What did they have to eat/drink? |
|---|---|---|---|---|
| Speaker 1 | ............................ | ............................ | ............................ | ............................ |
|  | ............................ | ............................ | ............................ | ............................ |
| Speaker 2 | ............................ | ............................ | ............................ | ............................ |
|  | ............................ | ............................ | ............................ | ............................ |
| Speaker 3 | ............................ | ............................ | ............................ | ............................ |
|  | ............................ | ............................ | ............................ | ............................ |

## 7 Make it more interesting

Adjectives and adverbs provide additional information and often serve to make texts more interesting and precise.

Rewrite this text to make it more informative and interesting, inserting words from the box in suitable places. Use each word at least once.

| old | enormous | essential | also | dusty | electric | as well | tiny |
|---|---|---|---|---|---|---|---|
| wooden | absolutely | just | surrounding | normally | foldaway | | |
| antique | quite | unexpected | pretty | useless | very | | |

I'm afraid my flat is untidy most of the time. There are piles of newspapers and magazines all over the living room, and bookshelves packed with books from floor to ceiling. But at least it's a quiet room and the table in the middle is elegant.

I sleep in the bedroom next to the living room, but I have a spare bedroom. It's full of junk and chilly in the winter, but there is an old fire and a bed which I keep for guests.

The kitchen is basic with a few items such as a cooker and a fridge. The one nice thing though, is that it is on the tenth floor of a block of flats with fantastic views of the countryside.

..............................................................................................................................................
..............................................................................................................................................
..............................................................................................................................................
..............................................................................................................................................
..............................................................................................................................................
..............................................................................................................................................
..............................................................................................................................................
..............................................................................................................................................
..............................................................................................................................................
..............................................................................................................................................

Compare your text with the sample answer on page 147.

## 8 Speaking partners

**A** Discuss these questions together.

1. Why do certain people find it very difficult to throw things away?
2. Do you think that people should occasionally experience difficult living conditions so that they have a better appreciation of the luxuries in modern life?
3. Have you ever had to survive in difficult conditions? What were they, and why?
4. What is the hottest and coldest temperature that you have experienced?
5. Which is worse, to be too hot or too cold?

**B** Try this guessing game. Think of something useful to have in a particular situation, e.g. in the desert, on a camping holiday, at a conference, etc. Your partner must ask you yes/no questions to try to guess what it is.

Example: *Can you use it to prepare food?*
*Is it made of rubber?*

## 9 Visual dictionary

Complete the visual dictionary for Unit 12 on page 123.

## 10 Reflections

This space is for you to make a note of things you have learnt in this unit. You can also use it as a diary to write about your problems and progress in English.

................................................................................................................................................................

................................................................................................................................................................

................................................................................................................................................................

................................................................................................................................................................

................................................................................................................................................................

................................................................................................................................................................

................................................................................................................................................................

................................................................................................................................................................

................................................................................................................................................................

................................................................................................................................................................

................................................................................................................................................................

................................................................................................................................................................

................................................................................................................................................................

................................................................................................................................................................

# WHO IS REALLY ON TRIAL?

| 1  We wouldn't get wet because ... | *if* sentences |
|---|---|

Put the correct verb form in the sentences which describe imaginary situations. Then complete the sentences in a suitable way.

Example: *Even if it* .....rained...... (rain) *heavily, we* ..wouldn't get.. (not get) *wet because* ..we would have our umbrellas and raincoats with us...... .

1. If you ........................ (lose) your passport, it ........................ (not matter) because

   ..........................................................................................................................................................

2. If someone ........................ (invent) a machine to travel into the future, it

   ........................ (be) fantastic because ...........................................................................................

   ..........................................................................................................................................

3. If you ........................ (not have) a holiday next summer, it ........................ (not be)

   too bad because ..........................................................................................................................

4. It ........................ (not matter) if a dog ........................ (bark) outside your window

   all night because ..........................................................................................................................

5. It ........................ (be) terrible if a distant relative ........................ (die) and

   ........................ (leave) you a lot of money because ...........................................................

   ..........................................................................................................................................

6. If I ........................ (lose) my job, it ........................ (be) terrible because

   ..........................................................................................................................................

| 2  It's the place where you ... | relative clauses; vocabulary |
|---|---|

Complete the sentences with a suitable word or phrase.

1. The ..................................................... is the place where you report a crime.

2. A ..................................................... is a person who commits a crime under the age of 16.

3. ..................................... is a crime which involves breaking into people's houses and stealing from

   them.

4. Jail is ..................................................... criminals are kept locked up.

5. A defendant is ..................................................... is accused of a crime.

6. A fine is ..................................................... convicted criminals pay as

   their punishment.

7. A witness is a person ..................................................... .

8. Imprisonment is the sentence ..................................................... .

9. A jury is ..................................................... .

10. The courtroom is ..................................................... .

## 3 The sound of money

**A** The sound /ʌ/ as in *run* occurs in many words with different spellings.

Examples: *run* /rʌn/   *love* /lʌv/   *enough* /ɪnʌf/

How many times does the sound /ʌ/ appear in these sentences? Underline them as in the first example.

1. The c<u>o</u>mpany is w<u>o</u>rried.
2. What is the punishment for drug trafficking?
3. The public don't trust the government.
4. We must reduce unemployment.
5. It was a tough decision for the judge.
6. We need justice for everyone.

**B** ▭ Listen to the sentences on the recording and repeat them.

## 4 It's similar and different

**A** Are these sentences logical? If not, correct them.

1. Mice are similar to rats, except that they are smaller.
2. Cheese is different from yoghurt in that cheese is usually liquid.
3. Burglary is a crime against property, whereas vandalism is a crime against people.
4. Wind is similar to a breeze except that wind is often stronger.
5. Perfume is different from eau de cologne in that it is more concentrated and usually more expensive.
6. Physical exercise is good for you, whereas fresh fruit isn't.
7. Blouses are similar to shirts, except that blouses are usually worn by men.
8. Cardigans are different from sweaters in that they usually have buttons down the front.

**B** Complete these sentences in a logical way.

1. Interpreting is similar to translating, except that interpreting ............................................................................

................................................................................................ .

2. Having a shower is different from having a bath in that ............................................................

................................................................................................ .

3. Taxis are usually quite expensive, whereas ..........................................................................

................................................................................................ .

4. Marmalade is similar to jam, except that ..........................................................................

................................................................................................ .

5. Going to the cinema is different from ..........................................................................

................................................................................................ .

6. ................................................................................................ , whereas studying

English is hard work.

**A**  How many ways can you remember from the Class Book of protecting your home from burglary? Write them down.

**B**  Before you read the article, check the following words in a dictionary:

| barbed wire | to deter | prickly | an intruder |

# Burglars in for a short sharp shock

No. 2 looks very familiar!

It looks prettier than barbed wire, makes less noise than an alarm and eats less than a guard dog. Police in Essex hope that the new anti-burglar device that they are promoting will soon be installed in the flowerbeds of its towns and villages.

Launched at Cambridge Botanical Gardens yesterday is a scheme for plants which will deter burglars. The police believe that if home and office owners put in certain plants, the life of intruders would be more difficult.

'Obviously it is a fun thing, but there is a serious side to it,' said a police spokesman.

Posters and leaflets advising the public which plants to choose will be available from police stations. Ray Veerman, horticultural consultant to Essex police, has made a list of 12 plants which are particularly prickly or uncomfortable. They include berberis, pyracantha, gorse, hawthorn and prickly evergreen.

They should be planted as a hedge to discourage burglars, or as an additional line of defence below a window. Offices and factories lucky enough to have a flowerbed are being advised that defensive planting could be that one extra factor, like a barking dog, that will deter burglars.

**C**  Complete these sentences about the text.

Police in Essex are ........................... the public and ........................... owners to grow

certain ........................... of prickly ........................... near their property to deter

............................ They believe that such plants will make it more ........................... for

intruders to ........................... homes and buildings. People who are interested in finding

out more ........................... about the scheme can get a ........................... from the

police station.

📖 Listen to the recording and answer these questions.

1. How often is a car stolen in the United Kingdom?
2. How many is that in a year?
3. How many cars are never recovered?
4. Many cars are stolen because the owner left it unlocked or with the keys in the ignition.
   How many?
5. Write down at least three pieces of advice that the speaker gives to protect your car against theft.

Combine the sentences using link words as in the example.

Example: *That's the woman. She won the medal. Then I interviewed her.*
**That's the woman who I interviewed after she won the medal.**

1. That's the place. The war ended.
   Then we got married there.

   .........................................................................

   .........................................................................

2. That's the box. It was behind the house.
   I found it there.

   .........................................................................

   .........................................................................

3. That's the dog. A boy fell in the river.
   The dog saved him.

   .........................................................................

   .........................................................................

4. That's the criminal. He stole some jewellery.
   It was found in the car park.

   .........................................................................

   .........................................................................

5. That's the present. Molly gave it to me.
   Then I went to Indonesia.

   .........................................................................

   .........................................................................

6. That's the town. I met Alan there.
   Then he was arrested.

   .........................................................................

   .........................................................................

## 8 Speaking partners

**Choose from these questions to discuss together.**

1. What forms of security (locks, alarms, etc.) do you have in your home? Is it safe?
2. Do you feel safe walking around your town at night? If not, why not?
3. Do you know anyone who has been burgled? Have you been burgled? What happened?
4. What are the most common crimes in your country? Which do the police solve most successfully?
5. Is law and order a common topic among politicians in your country? What promises do they make?

## 9 Reflections

This space is for you to make a note of things you have learnt in this unit. You can also use it as a diary to write about your problems and progress in English.

.......................................................................................................................
.......................................................................................................................
.......................................................................................................................
.......................................................................................................................
.......................................................................................................................
.......................................................................................................................
.......................................................................................................................
.......................................................................................................................
.......................................................................................................................
.......................................................................................................................
.......................................................................................................................
.......................................................................................................................
.......................................................................................................................
.......................................................................................................................

# 14

# TALL STORIES, SHORT STORIES

Put the verbs in brackets into the correct tense.

1. When I ............................. (get on) the bus I ............................. (realise) that I
   ............................. (leave) my money at home.

2. The room ............................. (be) in a mess because the burglars .............................
   (throw) everything on the floor.

3. When the children ............................. (go) to bed we ............................. (remember)
   that they ............................. (not clean) their teeth.

4. He ............................. (introduce) himself as Paul Senior but I ............................. (be)
   sure I ............................. (meet) him before.

5. Paul ............................. (join) the company last month. He ............................. (not say)
   much about his past at the beginning, but it soon ............................. (become) obvious
   from his behaviour that he ............................. (be) in the army at some point in his life.

6. I ............................. (rush) to the station but unfortunately the train ............................. (go).

7. When she ............................. (get) home, she ............................. (be) annoyed to see
   that her husband ............................. (not do) any housework.

8. I ............................. (never see) her pictures before, but as soon as I .............................
   (walk) into the exhibition, I ............................. (understand) why everybody
   ............................. (like) her work so much.

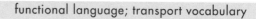

In the spaces below, write a suitable excuse for
being late in each of the situations.
Don't use the same excuse twice.

Example: *You are going to a meeting in a town fifty miles away.*
*You are travelling by train.*
**I'm sorry I'm late, but my train was cancelled and
I had to wait for the next one.**

1. You had to work late last night and didn't get to bed
   until 1am. This morning you are supposed to meet a
   friend at 8am.

   I'm sorry I'm late, but .............................................
   ................................................. .

2. You have to meet a business colleague for lunch. You are in a strange town and you only arrived yesterday.

I'm sorry ........................................................................................................................ .

3. You are meeting someone in the city centre in the middle of the rush-hour. You are travelling into the centre by car.

........................................................................................................................ .

4. You are going to a business meeting in a town fifty miles away. You are travelling by car and arrive one hour late.

........................................................................................................................ .

5. You are meeting a friend for coffee at her house, and you are on your bike.

........................................................................................................................ .

## 3  What could it be?

vocabulary: collocation

**What could *it* be in each of these sentences?**

Example: *It can take off, land and crash.*
         It *could be a plane or a helicopter.*

1. It can fly, sing and hop. ....................................................................

2. It can tick, stop and go off. ....................................................................

3. It can skid, accelerate and stop. ....................................................................

4. It can arrive, slow down and be cancelled. ....................................................................

5. It can jump, gallop and walk. ....................................................................

6. It can overturn, break down and reverse. ....................................................................

7. It can take place, be arranged and be cancelled. ....................................................................

8. You can tell it, listen to it, and invent it. ....................................................................

## 4  Find the right word

wordbuilding

**Complete the sentences using the correct form of the words in brackets.**

1. She is a very ........................................... and gifted child.   (imagine)

2. The man looked at me very ........................................... .   (suspicion)

3. The match was ........................................... because of bad weather.   (cancel)

4. His ........................................... was an accident.   (die)

5. Some people become ........................................... with work.   (obsession)

6. It's a very ........................................... book. You should read it.   (enjoy)

7. When I was at school we had to ........................................... passages from our textbooks.   (memory)

8. She was here a minute ago and then she just ........................................... . I don't know where she is.   (disappear)

9. They were ........................................... when she told them what had happened. (astonish)

10. The programme helps children to be ........................................... .   (create)

In your Class Book in Unit 14, you listened to a story about a face on a wall. In the story below, a face is also important. Read the passage and then answer the questions about it.

# I NEVER FORGET A FACE

## by Cyril Hare

I'LL TELL YOU A STRANGE thing about me – I never forget a face. The only trouble is that usually I'm quite unable to tell you the name of the person. I know what you're going to say – you suffer from the same thing yourself. Lots of people do, to some extent, but I'm not like that. When I say I never forget a face, I mean it. I can pass a fellow in the street one day and recognise him months after, though we've never spoken to each other. My wife says sometimes that I ought to be a reporter for the newspapers and wait about at first nights at cinemas, looking for all the famous people who go to see the films. But, as I tell her, I should not be able to do very well at that. I should see the famous man or woman, but I should not be able to say which one it was. That's my trouble, as I say – names.

You can guess that there's not a man, woman or child here in Bardfield that I don't know by sight. I've lived in Bardfield ever since the war. I like the place; although it's only forty minutes from London, there's a lot of country here. The village is over a mile from the station, and that's rather troublesome. But quite a pleasant crowd of men travel up and down to the City most days, and I needn't tell you that I don't know the names of half of them, though we speak to each other cheerfully enough.

Well, on this particular evening, I'd been kept a bit late at the office, and it was difficult to get to the station in time to catch the train.

There was quite a crowd in the train at first, but they gradually got off; and by the time we reached Ellingham – that's two stations before mine – there were only two of us left in the carriage. The other fellow wasn't one of the regular travellers, but I knew he was a Bardfield man. I knew it as soon as I saw him, of course. I'd smiled at him when I saw him get into the carriage in London, and he had smiled back. But that didn't tell me his name. The annoying thing was that I couldn't *place* the fellow, if you understand what I mean. His face told me clearly that he was connected with Bardfield, but that was all it told me.

Are these statements true or false?

1. The narrator believes he has the qualities to be a good reporter.
2. He is probably a businessman.
3. He recognises the face of everyone in his village.
4. He gets on well with the people he travels to work with.
5. He had seen the stranger before on the same train.
6. He recognised him but couldn't recall exactly where he had seen him before.

Now go on to Exercise 6.

## 6  I never forget a face (II)

📼 Listen to the second half of the story on the recording.

Which person does *he* refer to in these sentences? The narrator or the other man?

1. He talked a lot about himself. ............................................

2. He went to sleep. ............................................

3. He gave him a lift. ............................................

4. He thanked him. ............................................

5. He asked to get out. ............................................

6. He hit him on the back of the head. ............................................

7. He found himself in a ditch. ............................................

8. He reported a robbery. ............................................

9. He saw a picture. ............................................

10. He had committed crimes previously. ............................................

## 7  Film synopsis

Do you know the story of the film *Tootsie* starring Dustin Hoffman and Jessica Lange? The sentences below give you an outline of the story.

Hoffman played an actor who couldn't find work.
He heard about a female part in a soap opera.
He dressed up as a woman and went for an audition.
No one realised he was a man and he got the part.
He became very successful and famous.
He never told the rest of the cast that he was a man.
He fell in love with the leading lady, Jessica Lange.
They became great friends.
He couldn't show his true feelings.
He revealed that he was a man on a live broadcast of the soap.
Jessica Lange fell in love with him.

Write the complete story using the facts and some or all of these link words and phrases. If you know the film, include any other information you like.

| | | | | | |
|---|---|---|---|---|---|
| after a while | although | eventually | and | after that | then one day |
| at the end of the film | incredibly | so | but | | |

## 8 Speaking partners

**A** Before you meet your partner, think of a story from the following suggestions to tell him/her.

- the story of a film you have seen recently
- a novel or short story you have read
- a TV detective story or soap opera
- an interesting anecdote from your past
- a children's story that you like very much

**B** You have read or heard two stories about faces in the Class Book and the Personal Study Workbook for Unit 14.

One of you should tell the story of *The Face on the Wall*, the other tell *I Never Forget a Face*.

When you are listening to your partner, you can follow the story in the text or tapescript to make sure the facts are correct.

## 9 Visual dictionary

Complete the visual dictionary for Unit 14 on page 124.

## 10 Reflections

This space is for you to make a note of things you have learnt in this unit. You can also use it as a diary to write about your problems and progress in English.

# 15

# LOVE THY NEIGHBOUR

## 1 I've been waiting for ages

present perfect: simple or continuous?

Choose the correct form of the verb in brackets. If you think both the present perfect simple and continuous forms are possible, write *both* at the end of the line.

1. My brother has just ........................................ (return) from America.

2. His feet are wet because he has ........................................ (walk) in the rain.

3. I'm afraid I have ........................................ (lose) my coursebook. Have you
   ........................................ (see) it?

4. I've ........................................ (write) a book for the last eighteen months, and I've only
   ........................................ (finish) about six chapters.

5. I'm sorry I'm late. Have you ........................................ (wait) long?

6. I have never ........................................ (understand) why young people like rock music.

7. She has ........................................ (work) for this company for a long time.

8. My sister has ........................................ (be) in France for three weeks, but she hasn't
   ........................................ (write) to me yet.

9. I have ........................................ (try) to phone her for ages, but the line is always
   engaged.

10. How long have you ........................................ (know) her?

## 2 You promised to help

verb patterns

Find the correct ending for each sentence beginning on the left.

1. He thanked
2. He threatened
3. He congratulated
4. He let
5. He prevented
6. He made
7. He offered
8. He helped
9. He accused

a. to help me.
b. me on passing my exam.
c. me to get a job.
d. me for the present I gave him.
e. to dismiss them.
f. me go out whenever I wanted.
g. me of taking his pen.
h. me walk even in bad weather.
i. me from playing games.

*Dear Aunty Janet,*
*What a beautiful …*

## 3 More acts of kindness

Use the context to guess the meaning of the underlined words and phrases in these sentences.

1. If you see a <u>tramp</u> in the street, offer to buy them a meal or give them a bed for the night.
2. Give a <u>donation</u> to a charity you like and admire.
3. If you see that a colleague at work is having a really <u>hectic</u> day, offer to do some of their work for them.
4. Buy some chocolate and give it to some of the <u>kids</u> in the neighbourhood.
5. Stop and have a <u>natter</u> with an elderly person you know who lives on their own.
6. If you see someone looking depressed, talk to them and try to <u>cheer them up</u>.
7. <u>Give up</u> your seat on a bus if an elderly person is standing.
8. If you have <u>quarrelled</u> with someone, apologise and buy them a present.

## 4 Sounds and spelling – same or different?

Look at the underlined letters in these pairs of words. Is the pronunciation the same or different?

Examples:  *dr<u>i</u>ver and r<u>i</u>ver* **different**
*lugg<u>age</u> and cott<u>age</u>* **same**

1. l<u>ose</u> and n<u>ose</u> .........................................

2. thr<u>ea</u>ten and cl<u>ea</u>r .........................................

3. sh<u>are</u> and c<u>are</u>ful .........................................

4. sm<u>ile</u> and host<u>ile</u> .........................................

5. desper<u>ate</u> and congratul<u>ate</u> .........................................

6. acc<u>use</u> and ref<u>use</u> .........................................

7. prom<u>ise</u> and comprom<u>ise</u> .........................................

8. n<u>eigh</u>bour and l<u>ei</u>sure .........................................

Listen to the recording to check your answers, and practise saying the words.

## 5 A group of wolves

Read the text carefully. As you read, underline about five or six new words. See if you can guess the meaning of them. Then check them in a dictionary when you've finished reading.

# Wolves

The popular image of wolves is not a pleasant one. In children's stories they are often portrayed as cruel, evil creatures, and many people are brought up to fear and dislike them. In reality, though, they are rarely aggressive to people, and within their own groups in the wild they are extremely tolerant and supportive.

Wolves are, in fact, very social animals, and as a group their social structure is similar to our own, but often works better because it lacks destructive human emotions such as greed, envy and revenge. Well-established groups usually comprise about ten members, and they have a hierarchical structure which includes upper, middle and lower class. The upper class includes the dominant male and female, the middle classes generally consist of non-breeding adults, and the lower classes would include any outcasts and youngsters under two years of age.

This structure is not maintained through aggression. Quite often there will be a group display of active submission to the dominant male, and this is designed to confirm his status and the group's solidarity as a unit. Naturally, quarrels do occur from time to time, and they can result in fights which may look frightening to watch. But they are over quickly, no one bears a grudge against the other for the future, and they rarely result in serious injury. And the reason for this is, once again, the primacy of the group over the individual: if one member of the pack is injured, the effectiveness of the pack as a hunting unit is reduced. As a result, disputes are more likely to be resolved through displays of aggression rather than actual fights, and the overriding atmosphere of the group is one of friendliness and mutual loyalty.

When you consider that if a female has cubs, other females will produce milk in case anything happens to the natural mother, you begin to see that a wolf pack is a very cooperative and consistently stable society. And it is this same instinctive commitment to the group that their cousins, our dogs, have towards the pack in which they live today: our families.

**Answer these questions about the text.**

1. The writer thinks that wolves sometimes achieve more harmonious and successful groups than humans. Why?

   ...................................................................................................................

   ...................................................................................................................

2. Wolves quite often have displays in which members of the pack demonstrate they are below the dominant male in the pack. Why?

   ...................................................................................................................

   ...................................................................................................................

3. When wolves fight each other they rarely cause serious injury. Why?

   ...................................................................................................................

   ...................................................................................................................

4. When a female has a cub all the other females in the group produce milk. Why?

   ...................................................................................................................

   ...................................................................................................................

Garrison Keeler is a bestselling American author who has written sketches of life in a small town in America called Lake Wobegon. Listen to the story on the recording about the Living Flag, and complete the summary.

The idea of the Living Flag started in Lake Wobegon because a shopkeeper called Herman

Hochstetter had ordered (1)........................................................................

The first Living Flag was performed in (2)...............................................

The shopkeeper told everyone where (3)..............................................., and when it was formed,

they sang (4)..............................................................

After a couple of years, people began to complain about (5)..................................., and about

(6)....................................... because he (7)...................................................

..................................... They also wanted (8)............................................... So in

1949, one person (9)..................................................., and said that it looked

(10)........................................ As a result, everyone else (11)...............................

.................................. It took (12)...............................

**Write about the neighbourhood you live in, using this framework.**

- where the neighbourhood is and what it looks like
- the atmosphere in the neighbourhood
- any particular buildings or the style of architecture
- the neighbours, and how people get on with each other
- any special people or characters in the neighbourhood

Here is an example:

> *I live right in the centre of the city in a block of flats on the corner of a large, open square. At first sight, it seems a bit impersonal and the buildings are rather grey and serious, but around the corner in the side street, there are a lot of little cafés and shops, and the atmosphere is very friendly. Every year we have a carnival, and our neighbourhood has its own marching band and dancers, so that helps to create a special atmosphere too.*
>
> *My family has been living here for about thirty years, so we know a lot of other people in our building and we get on very well with the people who live on our floor. The most important person in our block is the porter, Pedro, who is trusted and liked by everyone.*

## 8 Speaking partners

**A** Show your partner what you wrote in Exercise 7, and tell them more about your neighbourhood, or about another neighbourhood you have lived in.

**B** Can you think of any acts of kindness that you have seen or even received yourself recently? Tell your speaking partner.

**C** Do you believe it is possible for groups of people to change the way they behave towards each other, as the article in your Class Book on page 101 suggests? For example, in a neighbourhood, a school or a workplace? Do you think it is a good idea?

## 9 Visual dictionary

Complete the visual dictionary for Unit 15 on page 125.

## 10 Reflections

This space is for you to make a note of things you have learnt in this unit. You can also use it as a diary to write about your problems and progress in English.

...................................................................................................................................

...................................................................................................................................

...................................................................................................................................

...................................................................................................................................

...................................................................................................................................

...................................................................................................................................

...................................................................................................................................

...................................................................................................................................

...................................................................................................................................

...................................................................................................................................

...................................................................................................................................

...................................................................................................................................

...................................................................................................................................

...................................................................................................................................

# 16

# YES AND NO

Each sentence includes a mistake or an example of non-standard English. Correct
and/or improve them, but keep the meaning the same.

1. They didn't saw me.
2. I told him don't go.
3. I'm afraid he hadn't a dictionary.
4. Young people haven't to do military
   service in Britain.
5. A: Is it going to rain tomorrow?
   B: I don't hope so.
6. They go hardly ever to the cinema.
7. He never has been there.

8. We won't probably see them before next week.
9. I didn't see nothing.
10. She heard anything but I'm sure there was a noise.
11. A: I can't understand this question.
    B: So can I.
12. He was unsatisfied with the course.
13. I am not agree with you.
14. I think nobody can come.

Complete the sentences in a suitable way.
Look at the examples first.

Examples:  *I wish* .I had my glasses............ ,
           *then I could read what it says.*
           *I wish* .I didn't smoke................. .
           *It's very bad for my health.*

1. I wish ......................................................, then I could afford that new computer.

2. I wish ...................................................... It looks as if it's going to rain.

3. I wish ......................................................, then I could talk to the French family next door.

4. I wish ...................................................... I've always hated curly hair.

5. I wish ...................................................... I would really like to stay in bed.

6. I wish ...................................................... The sun is burning my nose.

7. I wish ...................................................... It's so hot and smoky in here.

8. I wish ...................................................... I have to go in half an hour and there is

   so much still to do.

## 3 Agreeing with each other

**A** Read these rules, then do the exercise below.

> *So do I* is used to agree with positive statements.

A: I study English.★
B: So do I.

> *Neither do I* is used to agree with negative statements.

A: I don't read very much.
B: Neither do I.

> The auxiliary verb which comes after *so* or *neither* depends on the verb form used in the prompt sentence.

A: I *can* speak German.   A: I*'ve had* two operations.
B: So *can* I.              B: So *have* I.
A: I *didn't* see that film.  A: I lost my wallet yesterday.★
B: Neither *did* I.          B: So *did* I.

★ These examples show the simple affirmative forms, which have no auxiliary. You have to supply the auxiliary (*do/did*) in the reply.

**Agree with each of these sentences.**

Examples:   *I like Tokyo.*
            **So do I.**
            *I don't like storms.*
            **Neither do I.**
            *I haven't got much money.*
            **Neither have I.**

1. I can't fly a plane.              5. I've got a new car.
2. I don't work at weekends.         6. I don't get up very early.
3. I love swimming.                  7. I didn't go last night.
4. I've never been to New Zealand.   8. I don't speak Portuguese.

**B** 🔲 Now agree with the sentences on the recording. Listen and answer as quickly as you can.

Do it again, until you can do it perfectly.

## 4 What's the opposite?

**A** Form opposites of these words using *un-*, *dis-*, or *-less*.

| careful | ......... | honest | ......... |
|---|---|---|---|
| useful | ......... | obedient | ......... |
| successful | ......... | satisfied | ......... |
| painful | ......... | organised | ......... |
| helpful | ......... | satisfactory | ......... |
| tactful | ......... | reliable | ......... |
| thoughtful | ......... | pleasant | ......... |
| harmful | ......... | grateful | ......... |

**B** Rewrite these sentences to give them the opposite meaning. Make any changes that are necessary.

1. I was satisfied with the results.
2. The weather was fine so it was very pleasant.
3. My watch is reliable, so I don't need to check it very often.
4. My dog is very obedient; it does everything I tell it.
5. She's very honest; she never tells lies.
6. He's very tactful, so I'm sure he'll say something polite.
7. They were very grateful and they all said that my comments were useful and very helpful.
8. He's careful and organised so I think his work will be satisfactory.

## 5 When *yes* means *no*, and *no* means *yes*                    reading

Read the text and match the paragraphs 1–5 with these diagrams.

Many people believe that there is only one way to signal *yes* and one way to signal *no* – the head nod and the head shake – and that these actions are global in their distribution. This is close to the truth, but it is not the whole truth. In certain regions there are other, less well-known head movements that are used locally to signify affirmatives and negatives, and unless these are understood, travellers may find themselves in difficulties. There are five main head actions:

**1. THE HEAD NOD**   The head moves vertically up or down on one or more occasions; the down movement is usually stronger than the up movement. This occurs almost everywhere – from Eskimos to Australian Aborigines – and it is always a *yes* sign, never a *no* sign.

**2. THE HEAD SHAKE**   The head turns horizontally from side to side, with equal emphasis left and right. This is the most common form of negative response, and can mean *'I cannot'* and *'I will not'*, to *'I disagree'* and *'I do not know'*. It can also signal disapproval or bewilderment.

**3. THE HEAD TWIST**   The head turns sharply to one side and back again to the neutral position. This is half a head shake and means much the same. It is employed as a *no* sign in parts of Ethiopia and elsewhere.

**4. THE HEAD SWAY**   The head tilts rhythmically from side to side. To most Europeans this would mean *'Maybe yes, maybe no'*, but in Bulgaria and parts of Greece, Turkey, Iran and Bengal, this rocking movement of the head is said to be a replacement for the more familiar head nod. In other words it means *yes*, rather than *maybe*, and the movement is sufficiently similar to the more common head shake to cause some confusion.

**5. THE HEAD TOSS**   The head is tilted sharply back and returns less sharply to the neutral position. This is a special way of saying *no* in Greece and parts of the Mediterranean.

How much can you remember from the text? Try this test. Cover the text and then see how much of the box you can fill in. When you have finished, read the text again to check your answers.

| Head actions | Description | Meaning |
|---|---|---|
| 1. The head moves vertically up and down | ................................ | *Yes* almost everywhere |
| 2. ................................ ................................ ................................ | The head shake | ................................ ................................ |
| 3. The head turns sharply to one side and then back to the neutral position | ................................ | *No* in ................................ |
| 4. ................................ ................................ ................................ | The head sway | ................................ in Europe, but *yes* in ................................ |
| 5. ................................ ................................ ................................ | The head is tilted sharply back and returns less sharply to the neutral position | ................................ ................................ |

## 6 Saying *no* politely

**A** 🔲 Listen to the requests and invitations and refuse each one politely. Stop the recording after each one, say your answer, and then write it down. Use one of these phrases to begin each of your answers.

*Apologies*

I'm afraid I …    I wish I could, but …    That's very kind of you, but …
I'd love to, but …    I'm terribly sorry, but …    It's a bit difficult, I'm afraid.

**B** 🔲 Now listen to some suggested answers on the recording and compare them with your own.

## 7 Look on the bright side

Write some positive thoughts for each of these negative thoughts.

1. *Negative*
   I feel embarrassed when I speak in English because I make mistakes and my pronunciation isn't very good.

   *Positive*

   ................................................................................................
   ................................................................................................
   ................................................................................................

2. *Negative*
   Every weekend I go to the same places, meet the same people and do the same things. It's boring.

   *Positive*

   ................................................................................................
   ................................................................................................
   ................................................................................................

3. *Negative*

I'd like to go abroad this summer, but I have to work and study; I'd like to buy a new car, but I can't afford one; and I'd like to go out more in the evening, but I'm too tired.

*Positive*

..........................................................................................................................

..........................................................................................................................

..........................................................................................................................

4. *Negative*

There are so many words in English. How will I ever learn and remember how to use them?

*Positive*

..........................................................................................................................

..........................................................................................................................

..........................................................................................................................

## 8  Speaking partners

**A** Can you think of any situations when you say *yes*, but you would really like to say *no*? Tell your partner about them.

**B** When you are feeling negative, what kinds of things do you do to make you feel positive again?

**C** Before you meet your partner, make a list of about five things that make you feel positive and five that make you feel negative. When you meet your partner, say some of your things, but don't say how they make you feel. See if your partner has the same positive or negative reactions to them.

## 9  Visual dictionary

Complete the visual dictionary for Unit 16 on page 126.

## 10  Reflections

This space is for you to make a note of things you have learnt in this unit. You can also use it as a diary to write about your problems and progress in English.

..........................................................................................................................

..........................................................................................................................

..........................................................................................................................

..........................................................................................................................

..........................................................................................................................

..........................................................................................................................

..........................................................................................................................

..........................................................................................................................

# PACKAGING

## 1 A packet of biscuits, please

vocabulary: containers

Complete the sentences with a suitable container word.

1. There's a ........................ of coke in the fridge.
2. I bought a ........................ of toothpaste yesterday.
3. We always have a large ........................ of fruit on the table.
4. I've put the plates on the table. Could you bring that ........................ of water?
5. There are two ........................ of biscuits in the cupboard.
6. I filled the ........................ with water and started to wash the kitchen floor.
7. We usually buy milk in bottles, but the shop only had ........................ when I went this morning.
8. I bought her a large ........................ of chocolates for her birthday.
9. The assistant gave me a large ........................ for my shopping.
10. What did you do with that ........................ of marmalade?

## 2 How many, how much, how far

vocabulary

In the word puzzle, find fifteen more words to do with quantities, weights and measurements. They are arranged horizontally and vertically.

```
S K O K I N C H F X R
Z P E I D C O U P L E
Q I A L O E X N A I Y
U N W O Z B F D I H W
A T V S E V E R A L E
R P O U N D W E G O I
T Z L I T R E D K A G
E O R Q B P A S J D H
R N C O P A F E M S N
D M I L L I M E T R E
A H S E T R U M I L E
```

## 3 Building words and shifting stress

**A** Complete the column on the right with the correct adjective. Use a dictionary if necessary.

| Noun | Adjective | Noun | Adjective |
|---|---|---|---|
| power | .......................... | luxury | .......................... |
| simplicity | .......................... | glamour | .......................... |
| danger | .......................... | security | .......................... |
| mystery | .......................... | history | .......................... |
| elegance | .......................... | similarity | .......................... |

**B** ⬤ Now mark the main stress on each of the adjectives. Is it on the same syllable as the noun in each case? Listen to the recording to check your answers, then practise saying the words.

## 4 That's not what I asked for

Complete the letter below using suitable words from the box. You do not need all of them.

| | | | | | |
|---|---|---|---|---|---|
| balcony | complained | sincerely | heating | conditioning | faithfully |
| refund | discount | reserved | booked | extra | written | facilities |
| provided | included | accommodation | confirmed | available | |

9 Victoria Lane
Wexley
Nottingham

26 August

The Manager
Summer Tours Ltd
27 White Lane
Nottingham

Dear Sir

Holiday no HO56: Receipt no A1032

I am writing to express my dissatisfaction with the .......................... provided for my wife and myself from 11–24 August.

I .......................... the above holiday at your office on 16 February. At that time, I was promised a room with a private bathroom, air-.........................., and a ..........................; this was .......................... in your letter of 20 February (enclosed). When we arrived, the room given to us had none of these ........................... After we .........................., the manager told us your company had made a mistake, and unfortunately no other rooms were .......................... that week.

We were also surprised to find that the price .......................... continental breakfast but not English breakfast, which was ...........................

In view of these facts, I think we are entitled to a partial .......................... of the amount we paid, and I look forward to hearing from you as soon as possible.

Yours ..........................

Robert Brown

Read the information below, using a dictionary if necessary. Then go on to Exercise 6.

## DURING A 75-YEAR LIFETIME, THE AVERAGE PERSON IN BRITAIN EATS:

| |
|---|
| 18,271 pounds of potatoes |
| 16,761 eggs |
| 49,075 loaves of bread |
| 16, 341 pints of milk |
| 14, 571 pints of beer |
| 762 cans of baked beans |
| 18 pounds of dirt |
| 8 whole cows |
| 36 sheep |
| 36 pigs |
| 750 chickens |
| and uses 64 miles of toilet paper |

➤ Mississippians eat earth as a snack – you can have it smooth and sherbet-like, sweet and chalky or sour and metallic.

➤ In 1985, a South African man was taken to hospital having just eaten 53 toothbrushes, two telescopic aerials, two razors and 150 disposable razor handles.

➤ The heaviest object ever to have been extracted from a human stomach was a 5lb 3 oz ball of hair which had been eaten by a Cornish girl and was surgically removed in 1985.

➤ William Pitt the Younger (1759–1806) allegedly drank 574 bottles of claret, 854 bottles of Madeira and 2,410 bottles of port in one year.

➤ A psycho-neurotic 24-year-old American woman ate a five-inch iron bolt from her hospital door, which incredibly went through her intestines but broke the bed pan when she finally passed it.

➤ In Chicago in 1980, as part of an 'outrageous' contest, Jay Gwaltney, then aged 19, managed to munch his way through an 11-foot birch tree in 89 hours.

## 6 Sorry I got it wrong

📼 Listen to the recording of the text in Exercise 5. The speaker makes ten mistakes. What are they?

## 7 Letter of complaint

You went on a package holiday but several things were different from the brochure and promises made by the tour operator:

– excursions were not free
– babysitting facilities were not available
– the hotel was a long way from local shops.

Complete this letter of complaint to the tour operator, and look closely at the example in Exercise 4 before you begin your answer.

Your address ...........................................................
...........................................................
...........................................................
...........................................................

Date ...........................................................

Dear Sir

...........................................................................................................................
...........................................................................................................................
...........................................................................................................................
...........................................................................................................................
...........................................................................................................................
...........................................................................................................................
...........................................................................................................................
...........................................................................................................................
...........................................................................................................................
...........................................................................................................................
...........................................................................................................................

## 8 Speaking partners

Choose some of these points to discuss with your speaking partner.

1. What products in your country have a brand name that you particularly like or dislike? If necessary, translate the name of the product. Here are some goods to help you remember brand names:
   – cosmetics, perfumes, after-shaves
   – cars, bikes, motor bikes
   – pet food
   – children's toys or clothes
   – a range of tinned foods
   – soap or washing powder

2. If you had to provide a meal at a summer party for twenty people, what would you provide? Would you cook it yourself?

3. When did you last go on holiday, and what type of accommodation did you have? What facilities were provided, and were you satisfied with them?

## 9 Visual dictionary

Complete the visual dictionary for Unit 17 on page 127.

## 10 Reflections

This space is for you to make a note of things you have learnt in this unit. You can also use it as a diary to write about your problems and progress in English.

........................................................................................................................................................

........................................................................................................................................................

........................................................................................................................................................

........................................................................................................................................................

........................................................................................................................................................

........................................................................................................................................................

........................................................................................................................................................

........................................................................................................................................................

........................................................................................................................................................

........................................................................................................................................................

........................................................................................................................................................

........................................................................................................................................................

........................................................................................................................................................

........................................................................................................................................................

# HONESTLY SPEAKING

## 1 Get it right

**Correct the mistake in each of these sentences.**

1. I said her that I would be late for dinner.
2. Did she tell you she's going to last night's meeting?
3. I didn't ask her what was the problem.
4. He told it was very cold in Moscow at that time of the year.
5. She asked him if that he had been there before.
6. The policeman asked me what time did I get home.
7. He asked her did she need any money.
8. She told me that I do my homework.
9. We said we have to go out, so we couldn't go to the party.
10. She was telling me that her brother have a lot of debts.
11. He wanted that the hotel refund his money.
12. I promised to bought the flat.

## 2 How did they say it?

**Use the verbs in the box to report these conversations. If necessary, check the verb patterns on pages 102 and 159–60 of your Class Book.**

| | | | | | | |
|---|---|---|---|---|---|---|
| promise | admit | refuse | threaten | thank | congratulate | accuse |
| offer | praise | | | | | |

Example: *I will give you the money back, Maria – honestly!*
       ***He promised to give her the money back.***

1. Oh, you've passed your exam, Marilyn! Well done!

2. Here, let me do the washing up for you.

3. I think you are lying to me about this.

4. Thanks a lot – I really appreciated your help with this work, David.

5. If you don't finish this by six o'clock, I'll give the job to someone else.

6. OK, OK, yes, all right – it was me, I broke it.

7. I'm sorry but I won't look after your horrible dog ever again.

8. That was very brave, and you saved that child's life.

## 3 Compounds and word partnerships

**A** Combine words from the two boxes to form ten common word partnerships.

| inflation | trade | peace | political | foreign | multi-party | public |
|---|---|---|---|---|---|---|
| industrial | government | newspaper | | | | |

| policy | agreement | party | rate | minister | report | figure | talks |
|---|---|---|---|---|---|---|---|
| dispute | election | | | | | | |

**B** Now use words from either box to form the compound words in these sentences.

1. The transport workers are part of a very large ............................ union.

2. Dealers buy and sell different currencies on the ............................ exchange.

3. There's a big ............................ estate on the edge of town with about twenty different factories.

4. Mrs Thatcher was Prime ............................ for over ten years.

5. If you want to buy dollars, what's the current exchange ............................?

6. She's a ............................ relations officer for a large company.

7. One of the functions of the United Nations is its ............................-keeping operations around the world.

8. The next presidential ............................ will be in two years, and there is no obvious candidate at the moment.

## 4 Good news and bad news

Complete these sentences using a suitable opposite.

1. The Democratic Party know that the coming election could bring them victory or ............................ .

2. Some people will find the film uplifting, but equally others will find it ............................ .

3. Will England's hopes for success in the World Championship end in triumph or ............................?

4. When interviewing candidates for jobs, it is important to look at both their strengths and ............................ .

5. We are waiting to see if the discussions will develop into a dispute or end in ............................ .

6. We are fighting for justice after many years of ............................ .

7. Everyone hopes things will go right for the team, but in the past so much has ............................ .

8. He denied attacking his brother, but I think it would be better if he just ............................ it.

9. What will happen? Will it end in success or ............................?

10. We thought there had been an increase in the crime rate, but surprisingly there was a ............................ .

Before you read the texts, check these words in a dictionary if necessary:

> a white lie     to offend someone     an estate agent     a clairvoyant

**A** The people in the texts were all asked the same question: *Does your job involve telling lies?* Two people said *no* very clearly – which two?

### 1. Sir Bernard Ingham
**(ex press officer to Margaret Thatcher)**

You can't tell the truth all the time. You tell white lies to avoid offending people. You won't last as a press secretary if you are constantly lying. You try to answer as truthfully as you can, but you can't tell all that you know – of course you can't.

### 2. Susie Profitt
**(the manager of a dress hire agency)**

You have to lie in business or you won't succeed. I tell very big lies. I hate the dresses here, they're hideous, but if a client asks me if I like them, I say I do. But I am very honest about whether a dress looks good on someone, I wouldn't let anyone walk out of here looking like an elephant.

### 3. Karan Lavida
**(a clairvoyant)**

If you *don't* tell people certain things, it is lying. It obscures reality. Anyway, I don't get a chance; the information comes to me at such high speed I don't get time to make a judgement.

### 4. Alistair
**(an estate agent)**

In the old days before they changed the laws about the way we describe houses for sale or rent in advertisements, we told lies all the time. Years ago, when I was a junior negotiator, the drummer from a famous rock group lived next door to a flat I was selling. The buyers asked me if the neighbourhood was noisy, and I said I didn't know.

### 5. Sandra Grant
**(a car mechanic)**

There is no point in telling lies. My boss checks everything I do. Mechanics only lie if their bosses allow them to. I prefer to be honest because it saves a lot of heartache with customers. If they think they've been robbed, you can always show them the old part, but some are never satisfied.

**B** Read the texts again and answer these questions.

1. Did the mechanic say that lying is not possible for her?
2. Did the clairvoyant believe that if you omit to tell someone something, that is a form of lying?
3. Did the estate agent admit that he told lies now?
4. Did Mrs Thatcher's ex press officer believe that white lies were acceptable?
5. Did the manager of the dress hire agency tell her customers if she thought the clothes didn't suit them?

🎧 Listen to the speakers on the recording. They each describe a situation where they don't tell the truth.

Complete the table, and then check your answers with the tapescript.

| | Situation | Reason for lie | Result |
|---|---|---|---|
| Speaker 1 | .................... | .................... | .................... |
| Speaker 2 | .................... | .................... | .................... |
| Speaker 3 | .................... | .................... | .................... |

**7 She said in her letter that ...**                                      writing: an informal letter

Read this conversation between Nickie and Martin.

NICKIE:   What did Susan have to say in her letter?
MARTIN:   She said they were thinking of coming down to London for a weekend next month. Paul is attending a one-day conference just outside London, and Susan said she was hoping to get a couple of days off work. Then she could travel down to Kingston with Paul – that's where the conference is – and afterwards they could spend the weekend in London.
NICKIE:   Great. Do they want to come and stay with us?
MARTIN:   No, that won't be necessary because her brother lives just outside Kingston, and he has invited them to stay at his place. But she said they wanted to take us out for dinner on the Saturday evening if we were free.
NICKIE:   Sounds lovely. Which Saturday is it?
MARTIN:   Saturday the 15th. She said she would give me a ring later in the week to finalise the details. But we aren't doing anything then, are we?
NICKIE:   No, I don't think so. I'll just have a look in my diary.

Here is the beginning of the letter that Susan actually wrote to Nickie and Martin. Write the rest of it, including all the information from the above conversation.

> *Dear Nickie and Martin,*
>
> *How's life in London? We're finding it a bit of a culture shock living in Scotland after so many years down south – it's so much colder for one thing. But the people have been fantastic. Everyone has made us feel welcome, both at work and in the village where we bought the cottage. It's nice to get away though, and that's really the reason I'm writing. Next month ..*.................................................................................................
> .................................................................................................
> .................................................................................................
> .................................................................................................
> .................................................................................................
> .................................................................................................
> .................................................................................................
> .................................................................................................
>
> *Best wishes,*
>
> *Susan*

## 8 Speaking partners

**A** Think of a situation like the ones in Exercise 6 where you didn't tell the whole truth. Tell your speaking partner about it. Only tell them if you want to, though.

**B** Report to your speaking partner some/any of the following:

- the most interesting thing your English teacher has ever told you
- the strangest thing your husband/wife/girlfriend/boyfriend (past or present) has ever told you
- the funniest thing a stranger has ever asked you
- the most difficult question anyone has ever asked you
- the thing you most often ask yourself
- the thing you most often tell yourself
- the nicest thing anyone has ever told you about yourself.

**C** Tell your partner some/any of the following:

- the most difficult thing you have had to tell someone
- the most difficult question you have had to ask anyone
- the last thing you asked anyone before you met your speaking partner today

## 9 Reflections

This space is for you to make a note of things you have learnt in this unit. You can also use it as a diary to write about your problems and progress in English.

......................................................................................................................................

......................................................................................................................................

......................................................................................................................................

......................................................................................................................................

......................................................................................................................................

......................................................................................................................................

......................................................................................................................................

......................................................................................................................................

......................................................................................................................................

......................................................................................................................................

......................................................................................................................................

......................................................................................................................................

......................................................................................................................................

......................................................................................................................................

......................................................................................................................................

# PLAIN ENGLISH

## 1 Familiar symptoms                                                                        vocabulary: fear

Complete the sentences below using suitable words from the box.

| tense | feel | shake | dry | stammer | sweat | argument | thread |
| blank | anxiety | bite | | | | | |

1. A lot of people ..................... their nails when they're bored.

2. In some situations my mind just goes ..................... when I am asked a question, and I can't think of anything to say.

3. The boy's hands started to ....................., so I could tell he was frightened.

4. I was half-way through my talk and I just completely lost the ..................... of my ............................. It was very embarrassing.

5. In conversation she is usually quite fluent, but as soon as she has to speak to an audience she begins to ........................... and can't finish her words.

6. A lot of people suffer from ........................... and sometimes it can be difficult to understand the true cause of it.

7. I knew the interview was going badly and I could ..................... the ..................... on my hands.

8. I always drink a lot of water when I am giving a talk because I find that my mouth often goes ..................... when I'm ..................... and nervous.

Respond to these statements using either *should*, *ought to* or *had better* where appropriate. Don't use the same response every time.

Example: *I've got something wrong with my eyes, I think.*
 .....**You'd better have them tested.**.....

1. It's getting very late.
2. Oh, no! I've missed the last bus.
3. I'm having real problems finding a job.
4. There are too many people living on the streets.
5. My boss is behaving very badly towards me.
6. My flat is filthy and my mother's coming round today.
7. Education in our country is suffering because there isn't enough investment in it.
8. There's the door bell! I think it'll be the police!

Complete the text using either an *-ing* form or the infinitive.

I have recently managed ..................................... (overcome) my fear of flying. Until this year, I never looked forward to ..................................... (go) on holiday because I knew the worst part would be the flight there and back. I would do anything possible to avoid ..................................... (take) the plane. On one occasion I was even prepared ..................................... (go) from Paris to Moscow overland by train, which of course took ages. I would spend ages ..................................... (find out) about train services which would allow me ..................................... (travel) in a relaxed frame of mind.

However, at the beginning of this year, I heard about a course which helped people ..................................... (live) with their fear of flying. I did the one-day course and it really made a difference. The course tutor was a pilot who started by ..................................... (explain) the technical aspects of the flight, the noises and the turbulence. In the afternoon a psychologist taught us ..................................... (reduce) our fear by ..................................... (practise) relaxation techniques.

At the end of the day, there was a short flight. Most people were still a bit afraid ..................................... (get on) the plane, but everyone did, and although I can't say I enjoyed the flight, I was certainly better than I had been before. I concentrated on ..................................... (use) my breathing techniques and the flight was over very quickly.

## 4 Employees and employers

**A** Complete the table.

| Noun | Person | Adjective | Verb |
|---|---|---|---|
| employment | ..................... | (un)employed | ..................... |
| ..................... | applicant | — | ..................... |
| education | educationalist/educator | ..................... | educate |
| ..................... | governor/MP | governmental | ..................... |
| ..................... | ..................... | — | consult |
| interview | interviewer | — | interview |
| specialisation | ..................... | specialised | ..................... |

**B** Use words from the table to complete these sentences.

1. It was only a small advertisement but two hundred people ........................... for the job.
2. The government's ................................ policy is excellent for children between the ages of 4 and 6.
3. I've been ...................................... since I lost my job last year.
4. Our company isn't doing very well, so the management have invited a firm of ...................................... to give us some advice.
5. The company ........................... in computer software.
6. Some politicians have no idea how to ........................... the country.
7. The factory ........................... about 150 workers.
8. It was really embarrassing when the ................................ asked me about my previous job. I knew he didn't think I was a serious ................................ for the post.

## 5 Word stress, sentence stress

📖 Read the sentences in Exercise 4B and then listen to them on the recording. Pay special attention to the stress on words from Exercise 4A, and also the rhythm and pauses in the sentences. Repeat the sentences aloud, and if possible, record yourself. How does your recording compare with that of the English speaker? What are the main differences?

**A** Read the extracts below and match them with these categories:

1. a request for permission
2. an invitation
3. a refusal of an invitation
4. a request for a service
5. a refusal of permission
6. an apology

b

> Lord and Lady Bodwood
> request the pleasure of the company of
> *Terry and Becky Miles*
> at a party to celebrate
> 25 years of marriage
> on Saturday, 12 July, at 8pm
> at the Covent Garden Hotel.
>
> RSVP

a

> Dear Lord and Lady Ponsonby,
> It is with great regret that I have to inform you that I will be unable to attend the reception at the embassy on the 24th of September. The reason for this is that

c

> Dear Mrs Cathcart,
> I must apologise for my absence from the annual policy review meeting yesterday morning, but I was called away to a very important meeting at

d

> Dear Mr Crow,
> Would it be at all possible for me to take a week's leave of absence at the beginning of August? I appreciate this will cause you considerable inconvenience, but I can assure you that if it were at all possible to

e

> Dear Jacob,
> Since I am unable to get out easily at the moment, I would be very grateful if you could purchase the following items of food for me

f

> Dear Mr and Mrs Lisard,
> I regret to inform you that the bank is unable to grant your request for a loan of £6000 to finance improvements to your property. Can we suggest that you

**B** Now rewrite the underlined parts of the texts in less formal English.

Example: *Dear Lord and Lady Ponsonby,*
*I am sorry to say that I can't come to the reception …*

## 7 My mind went completely blank

listening

Listen to the speakers on the recording. They are describing how they felt before certain situations.
Make notes on:

1. what the situation was
2. how they felt before the event
3. what happened at the end.

Complete the curriculum vitae about yourself.

# CURRICULUM VITAE

**FULL NAME**

Surname _____

Forename(s) _____

**PRESENT ADDRESS**

_____

_____

_____

_____

**PHONE NUMBER**

Daytime _____

Evenings _____

**DATE OF BIRTH**

_____

**MARITAL STATUS**

_____

**EDUCATION**

School Leaving Certificates
(including dates and grades where appropriate)

_____

_____

_____

Higher Education Qualifications
(including dates and grades where appropriate)

_____

_____

**PROFESSIONAL QUALIFICATIONS**

_____

_____

_____

**PROFESSIONAL EXPERIENCE** (List jobs starting with the most recent)

| Position | Employer | Dates |
|---|---|---|
| _____ | _____ | _____ |
| _____ | _____ | _____ |
| _____ | _____ | _____ |

**HOBBIES AND OTHER INTERESTS**

_____

_____

_____

**OTHER INFORMATION**

_____

_____

_____

**NAMES AND ADDRESSES OF TWO REFEREES**

1.

_____

_____

2.

_____

_____

## 9 Speaking partners

**A** Ask your speaking partner questions in order to get all the information on their CV.

Example: *What's your full name?*
*What's your present address?*

**B** Have you had an interview for a job? If so, tell your speaking partner what it was for and what questions you were asked. How did you feel before and after the interview? Tell your partner:

– what the job was;
– how much you wanted it;
– how formal the interview was;
– who interviewed you;
– what questions you were asked;
– what you answered;
– how you felt before, during and after the interview.

**C** In your country do you have an organisation that makes decisions about new words and standards in your language? If so, tell your partner about it.

**D** Is plain language always a positive thing in your written language?

## 10 Reflections

This space is for you to make a note of things you have learnt in this unit. You can also use it as a diary to write about your problems and progress in English.

........................................................................................................

........................................................................................................

........................................................................................................

........................................................................................................

........................................................................................................

........................................................................................................

........................................................................................................

........................................................................................................

........................................................................................................

........................................................................................................

........................................................................................................

........................................................................................................

........................................................................................................

# 20

# ART AND SOCIETY

**A** Match the sentence halves.

1. A forgery is
2. A portrait is
3. A design is
4. A reproduction is
5. *Intricate* means
6. Scenery is
7. To *exhibit* means
8. To *illustrate* means

a. to put works of art in a public place for people to come and see
b. a drawing which shows what something should look like and how it will be made
c. the appearance of a place, often part of the countryside with beautiful views
d. having a lot of detail, often made with great artistic skill
e. a painting or a drawing of a person
f. a copy which looks like the original and is intended to deceive people
g. to provide pictures or drawings of something for a book, newspaper, magazine, etc.
h. a modern copy of a painting, piece of furniture or artefact

**B** Now write your own definitions for these words.

1. A self-portrait is ...................................................................................

2. A gallery is ...................................................................................

3. A landscape (picture) is ...................................................................................

4. To display means ...................................................................................

Put *a, an, the* or nothing in the spaces. Then check your answers by looking again at the text in your Class Book on page 139.

At another museum shop in ............ Musée d'Orsay, you can buy ............ pocket watch

copied from ............ one in Alfred Stevens's *Le Bain,* ............ copy of ............ Cézanne's blue

vase from his famous painting of the same name, and ............ glass and jug from a Dégas

painting. ............ keen gardeners can also purchase ............ pair of garden shears like ............

ones in ............ Manet's *Branches de pivoines et sécateur,* but that seems strange, as ............ same

tool can be found at ............ garden shop for a fraction of the price.

## 3 We've been sold a forgery

Transform these sentences to express a similar idea.

Example: *Someone has sold us a forgery.*
*We* **have been sold a forgery.**

1. The books were all illustrated by a well-known artist.

   A well-known artist ........................................................................................

2. Foreign currency should be declared when you arrive at Customs.

   You ........................................................................................

3. The artist has to do all drawings of the accused from memory later.

   All ........................................................................................

4. The public cannot usually visit private art collections without special arrangements.

   Private ........................................................................................

5. In Switzerland, they replace bank notes very regularly, before they begin to look old.

   In Switzerland, bank notes ........................................................................................

6. They shouldn't charge entrance fees to people on low incomes.

   People ........................................................................................

## 4 A self-portrait that's forgery-proof

**A** If a bank note is 'forgery-proof', it means it is safe from forgers. In other words, nobody can produce a copy of it. We can use *-proof* as a suffix with this meaning in a number of words. Complete the sentences using words from the box.

| bullet | water | shock | sound |
|---|---|---|---|

1. These shoes are ................-proof, so your feet shouldn't get wet if it rains.

2. The President drives everywhere in a car with ................-proof windows to be protected from possible assassins.

3. A studio has to be ................-proof in order to keep out all external noise.

4. My watch is ................-proof, so it should be OK even if you drop it on the floor.

**B** A self-portrait is a portrait of oneself. *Self-* is used as a prefix in a similar way with a number of nouns. Complete the sentences below with words from the box.

| control | confidence | service | defence |
|---|---|---|---|

1. The owner of the house said that the burglar pulled out a knife and tried to use it on him, so he took down his gun and shot the burglar in self-................ .

2. I was very angry and nearly hit the man, but fortunately I managed to keep my self-

   ................ .

3. Self-................ is very common in cheaper restaurants because you don't need to pay for waiters and waitresses.

4. The manager kept criticising his players and eventually they began to lose their self-

   ................ .

Read the letter from Vincent van Gogh (Dutch painter, 1853–90) to an English painter called Horace Mann Livens. They met when they were fellow students at the Antwerp Academy.

He sometimes uses non-standard English.

**Find answers to these questions:**

1. What does van Gogh think of Livens?
2. What is van Gogh's financial situation like?
3. What kind of pictures is he painting at the moment?
4. Is his mood optimistic or pessimistic?

Paris

My dear Mr Livens,

Since I have been here in Paris I have very often thought of you and your work. You will remember that I liked your colour, your ideas on art and literature, and I add, most of all your personality. I have already before now thought that I ought to let you know what I was doing [and] where I was. But what restrained me was that I find living in Paris is much dearer than in Antwerp, and not knowing what your circumstances are, I dare not say come over to Paris from Antwerp without warning you that it costs one dearer, and that if poor, one has to suffer many things – as you may imagine. But on the other hand, there is more chance of selling. There is also a good chance of exchanging pictures with other artists.

There is much to be seen here – for instance Delacroix, to name only one master. In Antwerp I did not even know what the Impressionists were, now I have seen them, and though not being one of the club yet, I have much admired certain impressionists' pictures – Degas nude figure – Claude Monet landscape.

And now for what regards what I myself have been doing, I have lacked money for paying models, or I would have entirely given myself to figure painting. But I have made a series of colour studies in painting flowers: red poppies, blue cornflowers and mysotys, white and rose roses, yellow chrysanthemums – seeking oppositions of blue with orange, red and green, yellow and violet seeking ... to harmonise brutal extremes. Trying to render an intense colour and not a grey harmony.

... With regard to my chances of sale, they are certainly not much but still I do have a beginning.

At the present moment I have found four dealers who have exhibited studies of mine. And I have exchanged studies with many artists.

Now the price is 50 francs. Certainly not much, but as far as I can see, one must sell cheap to get on. And mind, my dear fellow, Paris is Paris. There is only one Paris and however hard living may be here, and even if it became worse and harder, the French air clears the brain and does good – a world of good.

Yours truly,

Vincent

Read the letter again. Underline words to do with painting, and circle words to do with money and finance.

Look at the pictures in your Class Book on page 139. You will hear several people giving their opinions of them. Complete the table with a tick ✓ if the speaker likes the painting and a ✗ if they don't.

|  | 1. Tony | 2. Ian | 3. Patience | 4. Julia |
|---|---|---|---|---|
| Picture 1 (the bath) | ................. | ................. | ................. | ................. |
| Picture 2 (the blue vase) | ................. | ................. | ................. | ................. |
| Picture 3 (the café) | ................. | ................. | ................. | ................. |

Read this description of Alfred Stevens's *Le Bain* (see page 139 in your Class Book). Do you agree with it?

> There are a number of rather strange things about this bath scene, at first sight. For instance, the woman seems to be wearing some kind of vest and she hasn't taken off her bracelet or hairband either.
>
> And why has she got a pocket watch in the soap dish? It seems an odd place to put it. Obviously for this woman, a bath is a time for relaxation and pleasure: in the foreground there's a book open next to her, and she's looking dreamy and distant, as if the roses in her hand are part of a beautiful memory. Is she alone, I wonder?
>
> It's a very restful, peaceful and sensuous scene with wonderful subdued colours in grey-green tones. I find it rather beautiful.

Find a picture of your own, or use one from Unit 20 in the Class Book. Write a description of the picture, and say what you think of it.

**8 Speaking partners**

**A** Before you meet your speaking partner, find some copies of pictures that you particularly like. You could look in art books, or find postcards of paintings. You might even find an illustration in a magazine or advertisement that pleases you.

1. Show your pictures to your partner and see what he/she thinks of them.
2. Tell your partner what you like about the pictures, or why you chose them.

**B** If you have done Exercise 7, show what you wrote to your speaking partner and discuss it.

**C** Tell your partner about any of the following:

– pictures you have on display in your home, or in your workplace
– any ornaments you own that have personal or sentimental value for you
– any exhibitions you have been to recently
– any TV programmes to do with art that you have seen recently
– any public art that you like: for example, in public transport, statues in the street or parks, etc.

## 9 Visual dictionary

Complete the visual dictionary for Unit 20 on page 128.

## 10 Reflections

This space is for you to make a note of things you have learnt in this unit. You can also use it as a diary to write about your problems and progress in English.

..........................................................................................................................................................
..........................................................................................................................................................
..........................................................................................................................................................
..........................................................................................................................................................
..........................................................................................................................................................
..........................................................................................................................................................
..........................................................................................................................................................
..........................................................................................................................................................
..........................................................................................................................................................
..........................................................................................................................................................
..........................................................................................................................................................
..........................................................................................................................................................
..........................................................................................................................................................
..........................................................................................................................................................

# DARE YOURSELF TO SUCCEED

| 1 Letter of explanation | job vocabulary; past conditional; *should have* + past participle |

Fill the gaps in the letter with a suitable word.

14 Taylor Drive
Brighton
Sussex
29 June 1995

Dear Mr Carter,

I am writing this letter because I am too embarrassed to speak to you in person.

When I .......................... for the job as a trainee in the first place, I did not notice the reference to German in the ..........................
If I .......................... .......................... it, I wouldn't ..................
.......................... for the job. However, when you invited me for an .......................... and you asked me if I could speak German, I was very embarrassed and I'm afraid I .................. to you. In actual fact, I did study German at school, but I was never very good at it.

I know I should .................. .......................... you the truth, but if I .................. .......................... honest, you wouldn't ..................
me the job, and I would .......................... heartbroken. Since joining the company I have .......................... once again to learn German, but I'm afraid it's hopeless.

Now you know the truth you will probably want me to ..........................
at once. However, I would like you to know that I have enjoyed working here very much and I have appreciated the help that I have received from all my .......................... .

I am very sorry for what I've done.

Yours .............................. ,

Melanie Campbell

Organise the words into correct sentences.

1. not    I    job    worried    losing    am    about    my

   ......................................................................................

2. my    satisfied    she    very    with    is    work

   ......................................................................................

3. build    to    she    reputation    wants    up    her

   ......................................................................................

4. my    boss    on    I    with    get    well

   ......................................................................................

5. upset    let    that    she    down    I    very    her    is

   ......................................................................................

6. going    in    I    autumn    am    the    course    a    on

   ......................................................................................

7. she    into    when    burst    I    tears    her    told

   ......................................................................................

8. project    is    she    for    responsible    the

   ......................................................................................

The above sentences contain phrasal verbs, verbs and adjectives commonly followed by a preposition, and phrases which include prepositions. Underline them and write them down in your own notebook.

---

**3 I wouldn't have done that**                    past conditional

Read the text and decide if you would have behaved in the same way.

Pearl came from a wealthy family and although she had a very good job in management, she never needed to work for a living. When she was thirty, her grandfather died and left her a fortune.

She thought for a long time about what to do with it, then decided to do a number of different things.

First, she decided not to give up her job, but to keep working. She also decided to give some of the money to a charity for the protection of birds. She invested about a third of the total sum in a friend's rapidly expanding computer firm. She gave a small percentage to strangers who heard about her good luck and wrote begging letters. She spent some of it on a round the world cruise. She bought herself a modest holiday home in Jamaica. She didn't keep any of it in the bank, but hid quite a large amount of it in different places around her home: under the bed, in cupboards, etc.

Now write at least six sentences, saying what you think about each of her decisions, and whether you would have done the same.

Examples:  *I wouldn't have given up my job <u>either</u>.*
           *I would have thought about it for a long time <u>too</u>.*
           *<u>Unlike</u> Pearl, I would have given up working.*

📖 Listen and write down each sentence on the recording and then check your answers with the tapescript.

Repeat the sentences to practise your pronunciation of weak forms and linking.

Read the story then do the exercise below.

# JUST ANOTHER FARE

**BY IRVING STERN**

FOR 28 YEARS, 3 MONTHS AND 12 DAYS I drove a New York cab. Now, if you were to ask me what I had for breakfast yesterday, I probably couldn't tell you. But the memory of one fare is so vivid I'll remember it all my days.

It was a sunny Monday morning in the spring of 1966. I had stopped at traffic lights opposite New York Hospital, when I saw a well-dressed man running down the hospital steps. He waved to me.

Just then, the lights turned green, and the driver behind me blew his horn. But I wasn't going to lose this customer. Finally the man jumped in. 'La Guardia Airport, please,' he said. 'And thanks for waiting.'

After a few moments, he started a conversation. 'How do you like driving a cab?'

It was a common question and I gave him a common answer. 'It's OK,' I said. 'But if I could get a job making a hundred dollars a week more, I'd take it – just like you would.'

The man's reply interested me. 'I wouldn't change jobs even if I had to take a cut of a hundred a week.'

I had never heard anyone say such a thing. 'What do you do?'

'I'm in the neurology department of New York Hospital.'

I decided to ask for his help. 'Could I ask a big favour of you? I have a son, 15, a good kid. He's doing well in school, but wants a summer job. Now a 15-year-old can't get work unless his father knows someone who owns a business – and I don't. Is there any possibility that you might get him some kind of a summer job – even if he doesn't get paid?'

Finally he said, 'Well, the medical students have a summer research project. Maybe he could fit in. Ask him to send me his last school report.'

He looked in his pocket for a card but couldn't find one. 'Do you have any paper?' he asked.

I tore off a piece of a brown paper bag, and he wrote on it and paid me. It was the last time I ever saw him.

That evening, around my dining room table with my family, I told Robbie what had happened. He read the note aloud: 'Fred Plum, New York Hospital.'

My wife: 'Is he a doctor?'

My son: 'Is this a joke?'

After I shouted and threatened to stop his pocket money, Robbie finally sent off his report.

Two weeks later, when I arrived home from work, my son was smiling. He had received a letter from Dr Plum and was invited for an interview.

Robbie got the job. After two weeks' voluntary work, he was paid for the rest of the summer, doing minor jobs for Dr Plum.

He then worked at the hospital for the next two summers, and after Dr Plum wrote references for him, he was accepted at medical school.

Doctor Robert Stern, the taxi-driver's son, became chief registrar in obstetrics and gynaecology at Columbia-Presbyterian Medical Centre in New York City. He is now in private practice.

Some might call it fate, and I suppose it was. But it shows you, big opportunities can come out of ordinary encounters – even something as ordinary as a taxi ride.

Based on the story, complete this sentence in different ways.

Robbie probably would not have become a doctor,

if *his father hadn't ignored the car behind him.* ..................................................

if ..............................................................................................................................

if ..............................................................................................................................

if ..............................................................................................................................


## 6 Different lives
listening

📖 Listen to the two people on the recording and answer these questions.

1. What is it that each person does well?
2. What event was responsible for them starting this activity?


## 7 A letter of application
writing

Expand the key words into sentences. Then write the letter, using appropriate paragraphs.

27, Devon Terrace,
Walton,
Suffolk.
14 May 1995

The Personnel Officer,
ICC Ltd,
Horseferry Rd,
London W1.

Dear Sir or Madam,

I / reply / the advertisement / *The Times* / 12 May / company interpreter.
I / degree in modern languages / diplomas / Institute of Linguists / Spanish, Italian, German and Polish.
I / speak / little Japanese.
I / work / translator and interpreter / eight years.
My first job / be / Bank of Credit and Commerce / I / travel / managers / conferences and meetings / Europe.
1994 / move / British Water / I / be there / ever since.
I / attend / interview / immediately.
If / application / successful / I / need / give / present employer / one month's notice.
I / look forward / hear / you.

Yours faithfully,


## 8 Speaking partners

**A** Have you ever applied for a job? What did you have to do, and what happened? Tell your speaking partner.

**B** What kind of jobs require a good knowledge of a second language? And what degree of ability is needed in each case? Add to the list below:

1. Airline pilot: needs to understand and be able to use very specific language while flying.
2. Hotel receptionist: needs to be able to greet visitors, explain things, deal with their problems in the hotel.

## 9 Visual dictionary

Complete the visual dictionary for Unit 21 on page 129.

## 10 Reflections

This space is for you to make a note of things you have learnt in this unit. You can also use it as a diary to write about your problems and progress in English.

................................................................................................................

................................................................................................................

................................................................................................................

................................................................................................................

................................................................................................................

................................................................................................................

................................................................................................................

................................................................................................................

................................................................................................................

................................................................................................................

................................................................................................................

................................................................................................................

................................................................................................................

................................................................................................................

Unit 21  DARE YOURSELF TO SUCCEED

# FORCES OF NATURE

| 1 Things you're familiar with | *used to + -ing* |

**A** Based on your own life, begin these sentences with *I'm used to* or *I'm not used to*.

1. ..................................... driving on the left.

2. ..................................... working at weekends.

3. ..................................... waking up before
seven o'clock.

4. ..................................... staying in bed until ten
o'clock in the morning.

5. ..................................... wearing a suit for work.

6. ..................................... staying out until two or
three in the morning.

7. ..................................... drinking tea for breakfast.

8. ..................................... eating a large meal at
lunchtime.

9. ..................................... spending my holidays
abroad.

10. ..................................... sharing a room with
another person.

**B** Look again at the things you aren't used to. Do you think any of these things would
be difficult to get used to? If so, write them down here:

I would find it difficult to ...........................................................................................

.............................................................................................................................

.............................................................................................................................

Tell your speaking partner about this next time you see them.

| 2 Transformations | *if and unless* |

Rewrite these sentences using *unless*, as in the example.

Example: *If we don't go now, we'll be late.*
         **Unless we go now, we'll be late.**

1. We can't make a decision if we don't have all the facts.

.............................................................................................................................

2. I wouldn't open the door if I didn't know the person.

.............................................................................................................................

3. If it doesn't stop raining, I won't go out.

.............................................................................................................................

4. They will lose the election if they don't communicate better with the voters.

.....................................................................................................................

5. I won't hire a car if it isn't absolutely necessary.

.....................................................................................................................

6. I wouldn't work for a living if I didn't have to.

.....................................................................................................................

7. If they don't give us more money, we'll have to close the hospital.

.....................................................................................................................

8. She'll get ill if she doesn't eat more.

.....................................................................................................................

## 3 Parts of speech
word building

Complete the sentences using the correct form of the word at the end of the line.

Example: *It's the most important* .. **decision** ............... *of my life. (decide)*

1. Many people live in ............................ all their lives. (poor)

2. Do you ever suffer from travel ............................? (sick)

3. She's the most ............................ person in the company. (power)

4. ............................ doesn't always increase with age. (wise)

5. These tablets should ............................ the pain. (relief)

6. I think the company was ............................ because their products were too expensive. (success)

7. During an economic recession the first priority is ............................ (survive)

8. You should take plenty of exercise if you want to stay ............................ (health)

9. Noise pollution is one of the many ............................ problems we have to try and solve. (environment)

10. The earthquake completely ............................ the building. (destruction)

## 4 Text reading
pronunciation

⊂⊃ Listen to the recording and complete the text. Then check your answers on page 138.

It was ............................ on 8 February, 1971. The children ............................ but

I couldn't sleep, so I opened ............................ and stood looking out at

............................. There was a black sky ............................, but it was unusually

............................. Normally there were ............................ animals moving about

– snakes, lizards, squirrels – but ............................. I'm

absolutely convinced they knew something .............................

Listen again to the recording. Notice how the voice rises and falls. Repeat the phrases in the gaps. At the end, try reading the whole text, if possible recording your voice onto a blank cassette so that you can listen to yourself later.

Unit 22 FORCES OF NATURE

Read the text and complete the table.

| Foods that help you live longer | Reason |
| --- | --- |
| ............................................. | ............................................. |
| ............................................. | ............................................. |
| ............................................. | ............................................. |
| ............................................. | ............................................. |

# Foods That Help You Live Longer

**DR GARY FRASER**, an epidemiologist specialising in heart disease, has started to put nuts on his breakfast cereal. He and his colleagues studied the eating habits of a large religious group who neither smoke nor drink, and discovered that those who ate a small handful of nuts five times or more a week had half the risk of coronary heart disease of those who rarely ate nuts.

'Nuts, whether roasted or raw, but preferably unsalted are a good source of monounsaturated and polyunsaturated fats and vitamin E,' says Dr Fraser.

Researchers are finding out about the disease-fighting and life improving powers of everyday foods.

People who live in the Mediterranean countries are, in general, impressively healthy. Some features of their cuisine – the reliance on fresh fruits, vegetables and whole grains, for instance, are all part of a healthy diet. But others aren't. For example, there is the 'French paradox'. The French eat as much saturated fat as the English, but the death rate from heart disease for French men is only about 30% of that for English men. Some researchers say this protection from heart disease is largely because of wine. In southwestern France, the average man drinks two to three glasses of wine, mostly red, every day with meals. Most epidemiologists accept that moderate alcohol consumption – around two drinks a day – probably has a protective effect on the heart. But too much is obviously bad for you.

When many people think of Mediterranean cuisine, they immediately picture garlic and onions. Modern science is finding surprising medicinal powers in these. They contain many sulphur compounds which kill bacteria, fungi and viruses. Garlic also thins the blood, which may be good for reducing the risk of heart disease.

In Japan, green tea is a popular drink. Research done on mice showed that green tea reduced the incidence of certain types of cancer. The proportion of Japanese men who smoke is double that of British men, but they only have about half the lung cancer mortality. Perhaps the tea helps to explain why.

Scientists were surprised when they started studying the health of Eskimos in Greenland. They eat vast quantities of fat, but they have very low death rates from heart disease. One reason is that the Eskimo diet includes a great deal of fish – salmon, mackerel, herring and others – rich in fish oils. These oils appear to thin the blood, reduce inflammation and may protect against colon cancer.

'We have lots to learn about the foods that nourish and heal our bodies,' says nutrition researcher Herbert Pierson, 'but we have a responsibility to select foods with our brains as well as our taste buds.'

CD Listen to the recording. The speakers all went to stay in another country and had a problem getting used to something. Complete the table.

|            | Problem |
|------------|---------|
| Speaker 1  | .................................................................................... |
| Speaker 2  | .................................................................................... |
| Speaker 3  | .................................................................................... |

Below is an outline of a story. Read the outline, then go back and complete the story, following the instructions in the brackets.

By ten o'clock there were over a hundred people at the party, and all of them in one room. (Describe the room and the atmosphere.)

..................................................................................................................

..................................................................................................................

..................................................................................................................

I decided I had to get some fresh air, so I opened the french windows and went into the garden. (Describe what it was like in the garden at this time of night.)

..................................................................................................................

..................................................................................................................

..................................................................................................................

The peace and quiet was suddenly broken by the raised voices of a man and woman who were having a terrible argument. (Where were they and what was the argument about?)

..................................................................................................................

..................................................................................................................

..................................................................................................................

Fortunately the couple couldn't see me. (Why not?)

..................................................................................................................

..................................................................................................................

..................................................................................................................

I could hear everything they were saying and I began to feel very embarrassed. I wanted to go back to the party but I couldn't without being seen, so … (What did you do?)

..................................................................................................................

..................................................................................................................

..................................................................................................................

A week later, I saw the same man and woman in a café. They looked quite happy, but when the man saw me, he rushed up to me and said, almost in a whisper … (What?)

..................................................................................................................

..................................................................................................................

..................................................................................................................

## 8 Speaking partners

**A** Look at Exercise 1. Tell your partner what you wrote and why.

**B** Do you have any personal experience of any of the disasters below? Tell your partner about it. Don't talk about it if you don't want to, though.

- an earthquake or earth tremor
- a flood
- a hurricane
- a tornado
- a drought
- a storm at sea
- a volcanic eruption
- an avalanche

**C** If you have done Exercise 4, read the text to your speaking partner, then find another paragraph in the text on page 151 in the Class Book to read to each other.

## 9 Visual dictionary

Complete the visual dictionary for Unit 22 on page 130.

## 10 Reflections

This space is for you to make a note of things you have learnt in this unit. You can also use it as a diary to write about your problems and progress in English.

.......................................................................................................

.......................................................................................................

.......................................................................................................

.......................................................................................................

.......................................................................................................

.......................................................................................................

.......................................................................................................

.......................................................................................................

.......................................................................................................

.......................................................................................................

.......................................................................................................

.......................................................................................................

.......................................................................................................

.......................................................................................................

.......................................................................................................

# VISUAL DICTIONARY

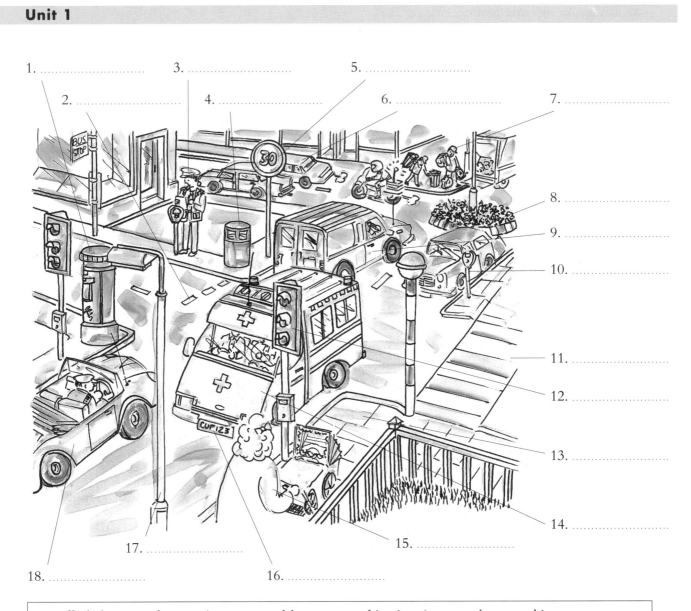

1. ...................
2. ...................
3. ...................
4. ...................
5. ...................
6. ...................
7. ...................
8. ...................
9. ...................
10. ...................
11. ...................
12. ...................
13. ...................
14. ...................
15. ...................
16. ...................
17. ...................
18. ...................

| traffic lights | zebra crossing | roundabout | road juction / crossroads | parking meter |
| van | ambulance | litter bin | postbox | streetlight/streetlamp | pavement | sports car |
| car overtaking another car | number plate | dustmen | traffic warden | road sign |
| pedestrian |

## MORE NEW WORDS

.............................................................................................
.............................................................................................
.............................................................................................
.............................................................................................
.............................................................................................
.............................................................................................

Label the pictures and give each group a title. Make a note if they are usually countable (C) or uncountable (U).

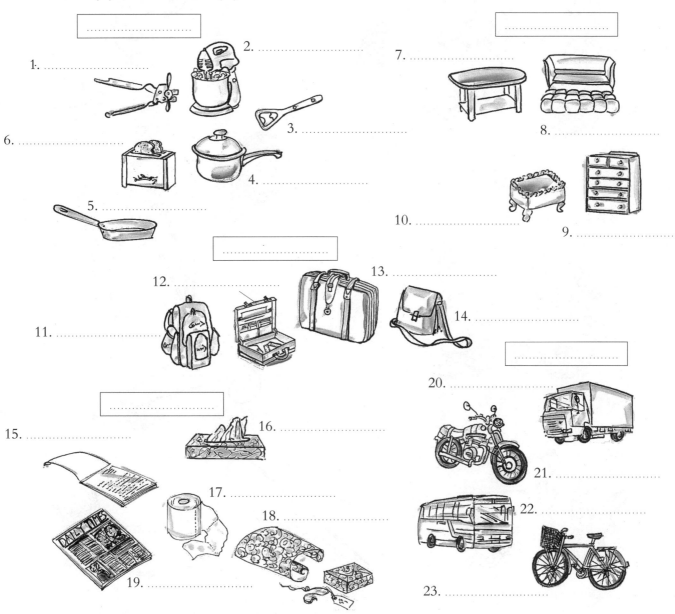

........................

1. ........................
2. ........................
3. ........................
4. ........................
5. ........................
6. ........................

........................

7. ........................
8. ........................
9. ........................
10. ........................

........................

11. ........................
12. ........................
13. ........................
14. ........................

........................

15. ........................
16. ........................
17. ........................
18. ........................
19. ........................

........................

20. ........................
21. ........................
22. ........................
23. ........................

| | | | | | | |
|---|---|---|---|---|---|---|
| lorry | toaster | newspaper | sofabed | bottle opener | coach | briefcase | saucepan |
| transport | toilet paper | bicycle | suitcase | kitchen equipment | paper | |
| chest of drawers | tin opener | stool | furniture | wrapping paper | coffee table | |
| food mixer | writing paper | luggage | tissues | frying pan | motorbike | |
| shoulder bag | rucksack/backpack | | | | | |

## MORE NEW WORDS

.............................................................................................................
.............................................................................................................
.............................................................................................................
.............................................................................................................
.............................................................................................................
.............................................................................................................

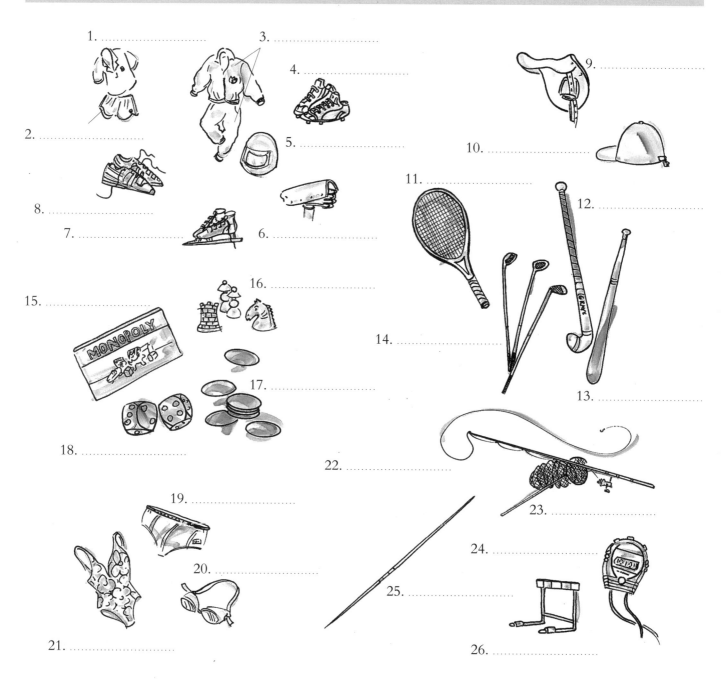

1. ...................................
3. ...................................
4. ...................................
9. ...................................
2. ...................................
5. ...................................
10. ...................................
8. ...................................
11. ...................................
12. ...................................
7. ...................................
6. ...................................
15. ...................................
16. ...................................
14. ...................................
13. ...................................
17. ...................................
22. ...................................
18. ...................................
23. ...................................
19. ...................................
24. ...................................
20. ...................................
25. ...................................
21. ...................................
26. ...................................

| | | | | | |
|---|---|---|---|---|---|
| javelin | swimming costume | golf clubs | helmet (2) | football boots | hockey stick |
| counters | fishing net | goggles | saddle (2) | fishing rod | baseball bat | tracksuit |
| chess pieces | trainers | board game | tennis racket | shorts | stopwatch | dice |
| sports shirt | trunks | hurdle | skates | | | |

## MORE NEW WORDS

...................................................................................................................

...................................................................................................................

...................................................................................................................

...................................................................................................................

...................................................................................................................

...................................................................................................................

Complete the network with these words. (One word can go in two different networks.)

| | | | | | | | |
|---|---|---|---|---|---|---|---|
| customer | girlfriend | neighbour | assistant | client | classmate | stepsister | mum |
| partner | boss | granny | fiancé(e) | colleague | supervisor | flatmate | relatives |
| niece | acquaintance | cousin | daughter-in-law | | | | |

Two of the words are only used informally. Which two?

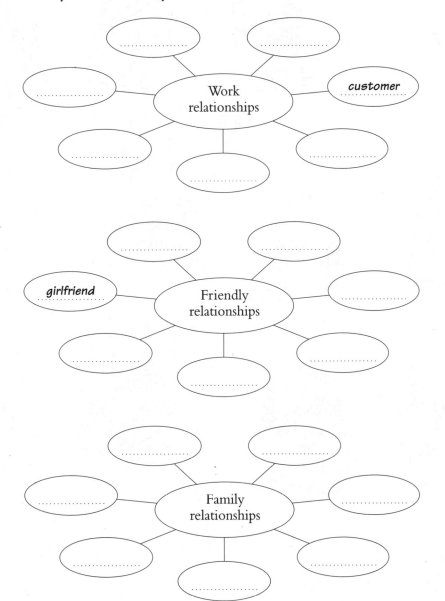

## MORE NEW WORDS

..................................................................................................................................
..................................................................................................................................
..................................................................................................................................
..................................................................................................................................
..................................................................................................................................
..................................................................................................................................

Label the subjects which are represented by the objects in the pictures. If you are interested in the objects, you will find the words in the Answer Key on page 144.

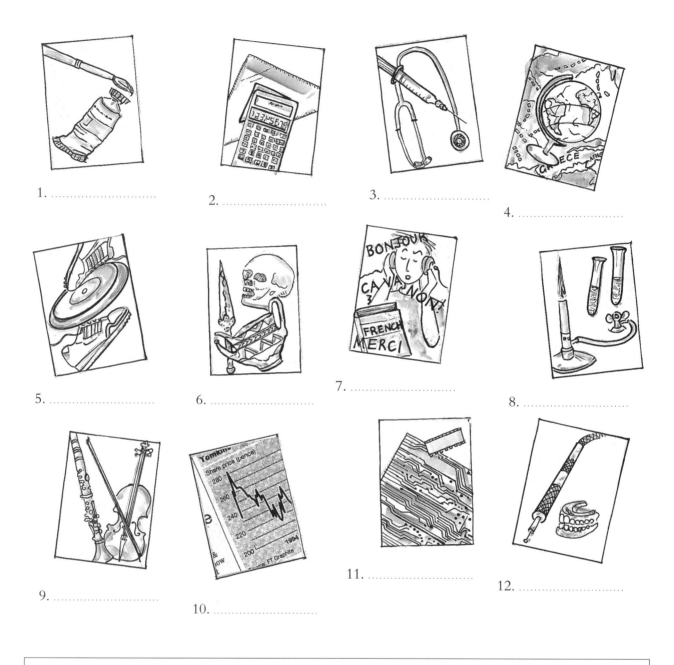

1. ...........................

2. ...........................

3. ...........................

4. ...........................

5. ...........................

6. ...........................

7. ...........................

8. ...........................

9. ...........................

10. ...........................

11. ...........................

12. ...........................

| art | dentistry | music | athletics | economics | geography | electronics |
| archaeology | maths | chemistry | foreign languages | medicine |

## MORE NEW WORDS

...........................................................................................................

...........................................................................................................

...........................................................................................................

...........................................................................................................

...........................................................................................................

...........................................................................................................

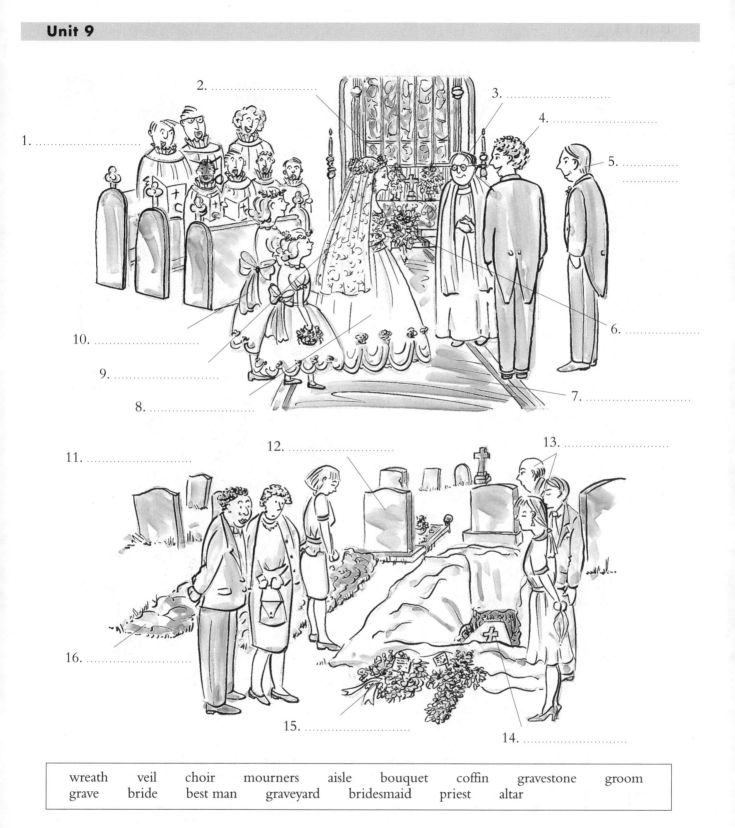

1. .....................
2. .....................
3. .....................
4. .....................
5. .....................
6. .....................
7. .....................
8. .....................
9. .....................
10. .....................
11. .....................
12. .....................
13. .....................
14. .....................
15. .....................
16. .....................

| | | | | | | | | |
|---|---|---|---|---|---|---|---|---|
| wreath | veil | choir | mourners | aisle | bouquet | coffin | gravestone | groom |
| grave | bride | best man | graveyard | bridesmaid | priest | altar | | |

## MORE NEW WORDS

.......................................................................................
.......................................................................................
.......................................................................................
.......................................................................................
.......................................................................................
.......................................................................................

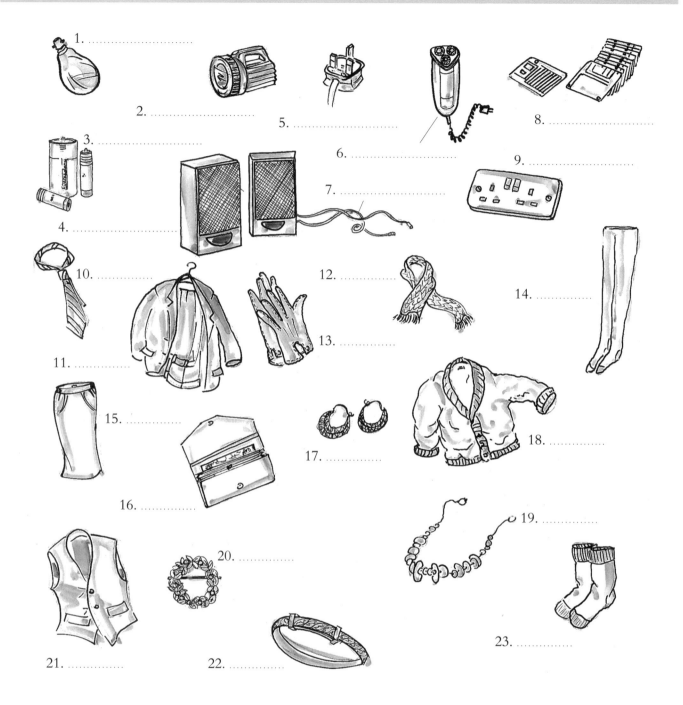

1. .........................
2. .........................
3. .........................
4. .........................
5. .........................
6. .........................
7. .........................
8. .........................
9. .........................
10. .........................
11. .........................
12. .........................
13. .........................
14. .........................
15. .........................
16. .........................
17. .........................
18. .........................
19. .........................
20. .........................
21. .........................
22. .........................
23. .........................

| | | | | | | | | |
|---|---|---|---|---|---|---|---|---|
| socks | brooch | plug | scarf | purse | torch | tights | lead | bracelet |
| cardigan | batteries | earrings | waistcoat | electric razor | | necklace | | light bulb |
| suit | gloves | computer disks | tie | speakers | skirt | socket | | |

## MORE NEW WORDS

.........................................................................................
.........................................................................................
.........................................................................................
.........................................................................................
.........................................................................................
.........................................................................................

1. ............................
2. ............................
3. ............................
4. ............................
5. ............................
6. ............................
7. ............................
8. ............................
9. ............................
10. ............................
11. ............................
12. ............................
13. ............................
14. ............................
15. ............................
16. ............................
17. ............................
18. ............................
19. ............................

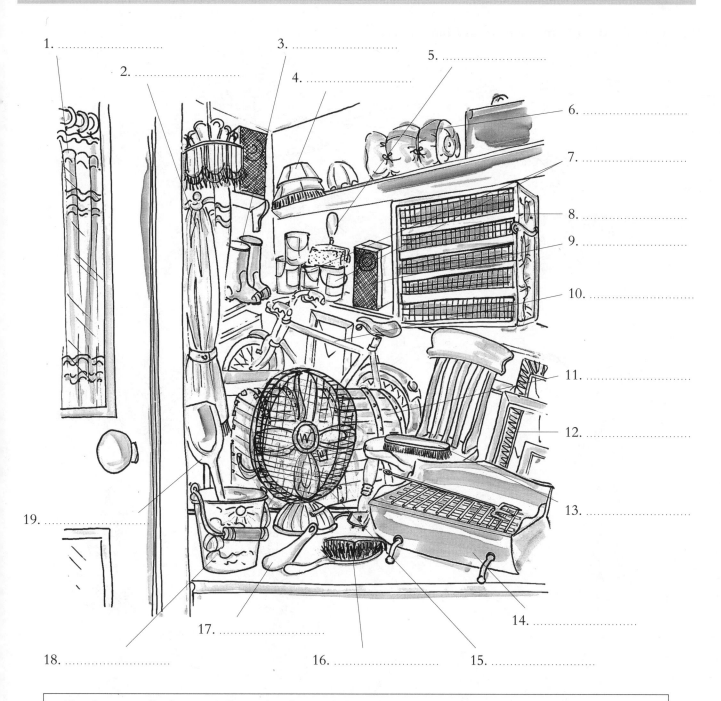

| | | | | | | |
|---|---|---|---|---|---|---|
| shoehorn | bucket | bike | spade | sleeping bag | barbecue | beach umbrella |
| picture frame | trunk | paint roller | hi-fi speaker | lampshade | electric fan | |
| brush and comb | clothes brush | foldaway bed | curtain | wellington boots | | |
| tins of paint | | | | | | |

## MORE NEW WORDS

................................................................................
................................................................................
................................................................................
................................................................................
................................................................................
................................................................................

Describe the actions using words from the box.

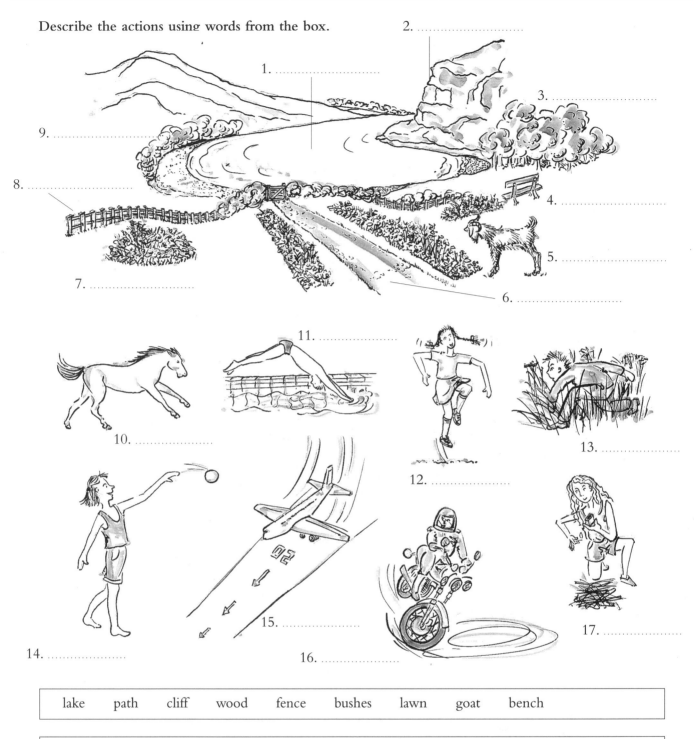

1. .........................

2. .........................

3. .........................

4. .........................

5. .........................

6. .........................

7. .........................

8. .........................

9. .........................

10. .........................

11. .........................

12. .........................

13. .........................

14. .........................

15. .........................

16. .........................

17. .........................

| lake | path | cliff | wood | fence | bushes | lawn | goat | bench |

| land | hop | light | gallop | creep | throw | skid | dive |

## MORE NEW WORDS

.................................................................................................

.................................................................................................

.................................................................................................

.................................................................................................

.................................................................................................

.................................................................................................

All the people in this picture are strangers to each other. In other words, people are committing acts of kindness. How many can you name?

1. ..........................    3. ..........................

2. ..........................    4. ..........................

5. ..........................

6. ..........................

7. ..........................

8. ..........................    9. ..........................    10. ..........................

## MORE NEW WORDS

..................................................................................................
..................................................................................................
..................................................................................................
..................................................................................................
..................................................................................................

**A** Complete the diagrams with opposites.

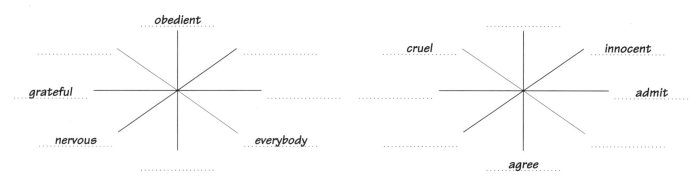

**B** Put other adverbs of frequency in a suitable place on the scale.

never                                         sometimes
_____

| hardly ever    occasionally    rarely    always    quite often    seldom    often |

**C** Complete the sets.

| | | |
|---|---|---|
| 1. ................... | ................... | dinner |
| 2. ................... | ................... | dessert |
| 3. ................... | ................... | university |
| 4. child | ................... | ................... |
| 5. ................... | ................... | hour |
| 6. ................... | decade | ................... |
| 7. beginning | ................... | ................... |

| minute    middle    breakfast    adolescent    end    second    primary school    year |
| main course    century    lunch    adult    starter    secondary school |

## MORE NEW WORDS

.................................................................................................................

.................................................................................................................

.................................................................................................................

.................................................................................................................

.................................................................................................................

.................................................................................................................

Fill the gaps with words from the two columns. You will need to use several words twice.

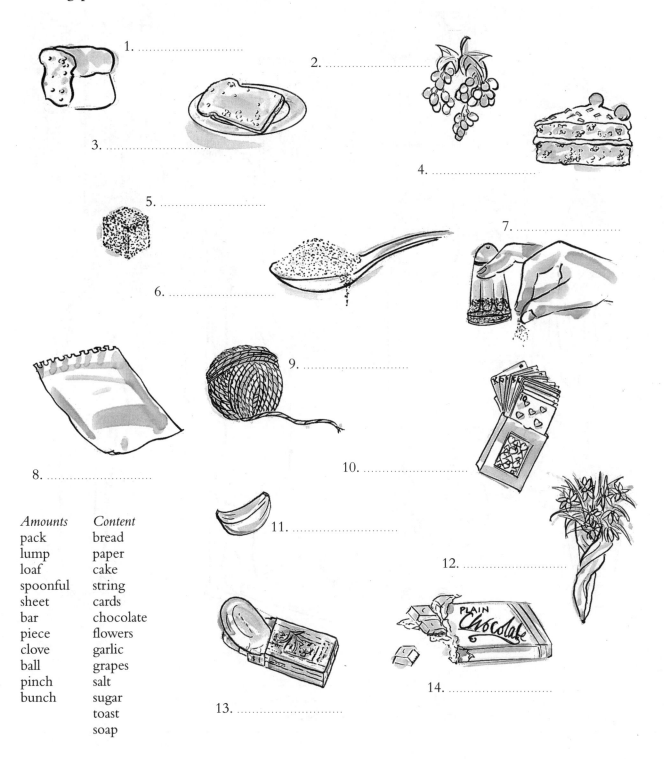

1. ...........................

2. ...........................

3. ...........................

4. ...........................

5. ...........................

6. ...........................

7. ...........................

8. ...........................

9. ...........................

10. ...........................

11. ...........................

12. ...........................

13. ...........................

14. ...........................

| Amounts | Content |
|---------|---------|
| pack | bread |
| lump | paper |
| loaf | cake |
| spoonful | string |
| sheet | cards |
| bar | chocolate |
| piece | flowers |
| clove | garlic |
| ball | grapes |
| pinch | salt |
| bunch | sugar |
| | toast |
| | soap |

## MORE NEW WORDS

..................................................................................................

..................................................................................................

..................................................................................................

..................................................................................................

..................................................................................................

..................................................................................................

1. .....................
2. .....................
3. .....................
4. .....................
5. .....................
6. .....................
7. .....................
8. .....................
9. .....................
10. .....................
11. .....................
12. .....................

SH☺P

---

artist    sculpture    postcards    jewellery    cartoon    abstract painting    vase
portrait    jug    self-portrait    statue    landscape

## MORE NEW WORDS

.............................................................................................................
.............................................................................................................
.............................................................................................................
.............................................................................................................
.............................................................................................................
.............................................................................................................

1. ........................

2. ........................

3. ........................

4. ........................

5. ........................

6. ........................

7. ........................

8. ........................

9. ........................

10. ........................

11. ........................

12. ........................

13. ........................

14. ........................

15. ........................

| | | | | | | |
|---|---|---|---|---|---|---|
| gliding | birdwatching | surfing | hang gliding | horseriding | abseiling | parachuting |
| camping | water skiing | canoeing | cycling | rock climbing | sailing | hiking |
| windsurfing | | | | | | |

## MORE NEW WORDS

............................................................

............................................................

............................................................

............................................................

............................................................

............................................................

Label the pictures and give each group a title.

1. .......................

2. .......................

3. .......................

4. .......................

5. .......................

6. .......................

7. .......................

8. .......................

9. .......................

10. .......................

11. .......................

12. .......................

13. .......................

14. .......................

15. .......................

16. .......................

17. .......................

18. .......................

19. .......................

| | | | | | | | |
|---|---|---|---|---|---|---|---|
| mouse | mammals | wasp | squirrel | insects | bee | rabbit | frog | fox |
| mosquito | rat | ant | donkey | crocodile | cockroach | reptiles | tortoise |
| lizard | fly | snake | spider | beetle |

## MORE NEW WORDS

.............................................................

.............................................................

.............................................................

.............................................................

.............................................................

.............................................................

# TAPESCRIPTS

## 1 LOOKING BACK AND LOOKING FORWARD

### 4 Word stress in compounds

traffic jam   primary school   central heating   zebra crossing
false teeth   income tax   air conditioning   post office
parking meter   credit card   car park   washing machine
compact disc

### 6 Looking back: recent history

AMBROSE: Lorelei, what can you remember about the year 1981?

LORELEI: Hmm, Ambrose, I don't remember a lot; it was many years ago, and I was very young. Let me think. Let's see: Reagan became the 40th President of the United States; um, I think they launched the space shuttle for the first time,

AMBROSE: That's right, yes, they did.

LORELEI: The Formula One Championship was won by Nelson Piquet; and I think there were assassination attempts on the Pope and on, er, on President Reagan.

AMBROSE: Right.

LORELEI: Someone else was assassinated. Anwar Sadat was assassinated … and I think also, er, that was the year Elvis Presley died.

AMBROSE: Er, no. No, it wasn't actually. You're wrong there.

LORELEI: Am I?

AMBROSE: Hmm.

AMBROSE: Juliet, tell me, what can you remember about the year 1985?

JULIET: Well, Ambrose, um, it was the year in which Gorbachev became leader of the Soviet Union. Um, also that year there was the terrible riot in Brussels in the Heysel Stadium, when the British football fans rioted …

AMBROSE: Oh, yes that's right.

JULIET: Ah, and also it was the year that, er, Bob Geldof organised the Live Aid concert which raised about £40 million. And the German tennis player, Boris Becker, he won Wimbledon for the first time in that year …

AMBROSE: Yeah.

JULIET: And … I think it was the year of the Los Angeles Olympics …

AMBROSE: Ah, no, no, actually that's not right. It wasn't 1985 because it's every four years, the Olympics, isn't it?

JULIET: Yeah …

AMBROSE: Um, so I think you'll find it was the year … well, it was either the year after or the year before.

JULIET: Yes, yes, you're right. I think you're right there – OK, and, er, what else was there? Oh, yes, *Out of Africa*. *Out of Africa* won, er, best film in the Oscars award, in the Oscar ceremony.

AMBROSE: Yes, yes, it did; you're quite right.

AMBROSE: Dominic, what do you remember about the year 1989?

DOMINIC: 1989, let me see, … well, I suppose the greatest significance of that year was, um, that the Berlin Wall came down. That was really the first tangible sign of the end of the Cold War, and, er, paved the way for the reunification of Germany. Um, I think also Margaret Thatcher resigned that year.

AMBROSE: Um, was it? No, I don't think it was, actually, I think it was …

DOMINIC: Was it 1990?

AMBROSE: … I think it was the year after.

DOMINIC: Ah, yes, yes.

AMBROSE: The uh, the end of the next year.

DOMINIC: Also, um, Emperor Hirohito died, leaving the way for Akihito to take over. Um, George Bush became President of the USA; he was of course Vice-President to Reagan for eight years before …

AMBROSE: That's right.

DOMINIC: So that was the third term for the Republicans. Um, there was also a huge earthquake in Tadzikistan, I believe. Tens of thousands of people died, very tragic.

AMBROSE: Hmm.

## 2 HOW DOES THAT SOUND?

### 5 Weak forms

1. She comes from Japan but lives in Italy.
2. He's a professor of Arabic.
3. The accommodation was very comfortable.
4. The weather's not very reliable.
5. She made a career as a photographer.
6. Do you need a safety certificate for that machine?

### 7 Where would you hear it?

1. Ladies and gentlemen, we will shortly be arriving at Kings Cross Station. We hope you have had a pleasant journey and apologise for the delay. Please remember to take all your valuables with you. Thank you for travelling on British Rail.

2. Good afternoon, ladies and gentlemen. Welcome to our gold spot sale day. There are special reductions on any goods that have a special gold spot on them. Many of these extra bargains are in china and household goods. Please note that at 11.30 there will be a fashion show in the casual daywear department on the first floor.

3. Ladies and gentlemen, we will be landing at Gatwick Airport in a few moments. Will you please ensure that your seat belt is fastened and your seat is in the upright position. May we remind you that smoking is not permitted until you are in the airport building. Thank you.

4. Your attention please, ladies and gentlemen. This is a security alert. Would all passengers please pass immediately through customs without collecting their luggage and exit via the main door. Please assemble on the grass verge opposite the entrance. You will be able to return to collect your luggage once the alert is over.

5. Ladies and gentlemen. The building will be closing in five minutes. Please make your way towards the exit. The gift shop remains open for another half hour. The gallery will be open again at 9.00 am tomorrow morning.

# 3 GAMES PEOPLE PLAY

## 3 A wall of sound

1. It's a kind of animal.
2. You need a lot of skill.
3. The rules are difficult at first.
4. I got it from a shop in Athens.
5. I'm optimistic about the future.
6. She didn't win anything at all.
7. He gave it up at the end of last week.
8. I'm not worried about it at the moment.

## 4 *Full of skill, or skilful?*

1. Joe – he just finds everything so boring. He doesn't go out, he doesn't want to meet people, he doesn't want to learn new things. I don't know …
2. You know, whenever anyone comes to the house, Sue just runs away and shuts herself in the bathroom till they have gone. She seems to be frightened of people – doesn't want to talk to them.
3. Mark is incredible really. You can ask him anything at all about English grammar and he can tell you the answer. I think he's better than a grammar book!
4. Jane always wants to be the best. She hates it if other people do better than her, and she loves any kind of game where she can have a chance to win.
5. The great thing about Marta is that she always looks at the positive things in life. Even when everything is going badly all around her, she still manages to find some good in it.
6. Lino had a job interview last week. He didn't seem at all worried, as usual. He seems to think they will offer him the job. He's always like that.
7. Alana doesn't seem to take an interest in her work; it must be terrible for her doing the same thing, hour after hour, day after day. I don't know how she carries on.
8. Julian is terribly clever with his hands. He can make delicate, complicated little sculptures and he can also paint beautifully.

# 4 NEWSPAPERS AND MAGAZINES

## 6 What do you read?

1. I like to read the *Reader's Digest* every month, because it has positive stories that I always find inspiring. I also like to read *Marie Claire* because of the fashion, the cooking and the cosmetic ads.
2. I like to read quite a lot of women's magazines, like *Elle* or *Cosmopolitan*, but my favourite is *Marie Claire*, because I think it has really good features in it and not too many advertisements, and I like the horoscopes and, um, the fashion pages. And I also like *Time Out* because it tells you what's happening in London, and what's on at the cinema, and about exhibitions, etc.
3. I like to read, um, *Body Builder* which is a weekly body building magazine, because I'm very into, er, getting myself into shape, really. And, er, I spend a lot of time in the gym, er, training, and I enter quite a few competitions, so obviously it gives me a tip on the latest fashions and techniques in, um, in getting your body into shape.
4. I buy, er, *Time Out* every week, mainly for the listings and reviews about cinema and theatre. I also enjoy reading the comment and editorial. They don't always agree with my political views, but, erm, it's very interesting reading. I also look at, um, *Hello!* I say look at, because I don't so much read it as look at the pictures. There's, er, only photographs. It's the sort of magazine I think that I wouldn't buy, but it's good for waiting rooms, because you can pick it up and put it down any time.

# 5 RELATIONSHIPS

## 4 Consonants

### A

A: What's your father's name?
B: My father? His name's Christopher.
A: What's your grandmother's name?
B: My grandmother? Her name's Marcia.

### B

1. What's your father's name?
2. What's your grandmother's name?
3. What's your grandfather's name?
4. What's your mother's name?
5. What's your teacher's name?
6. What's your doctor's name?
7. What's your best friend's name?
8. What are your brother and sisters' names?

## 5 I was the youngest

A: Well, my father is called James, and his wife (my mother) is Ann. Now, on my father's side, I've got one uncle, who is called Bob, and an auntie, who is called Christine, who lives in Australia. Um, on my mother's side I have an Auntie Barbara, and she is married with three children.

Um, still living, on the grandparents, I've got, um, my grandma whose name is Dorothy Ford – that's my father's mother, and on my mother's side, I've got my grandma who is called Phyllis Salter.

And then I've got two sisters. I'm the oldest, and I've got two younger sisters: one is called Celia, and she's two years younger than me, and then the youngest in the family is Susanne.

B: My mother's mother, that is my grandmother, was French, and she had four daughters. They were Jackie, Pat, Betty and Shirley. My father's mother had four sons: that was Peter, Tony, Brian and Michael. Michael is my father and Betty is my mother. They then had six children, so I have four sisters and one brother. Er, one of my sisters has a baby girl, so that means I have one niece. And each of my father's brothers had many children also. Two of them had six children each, and one had one son.

On my mother's side there are a further six cousins.

# 6 LIFE'S LITTLE CHORES

## 6 Guess what she's talking about

1.
A: You do this in a car …
B: Drive.
A: Erm, well, before you start driving …
B: Er, get in, get in the car …
A: Erm …
B: Before I start driving, turn on the engine?
A: No; in Britain you have to do it by law.
B: Oh, um, put on your seat belt.
A: That's right, fasten your seat belt.
B: Fasten your seat belt.
2.
A: You do this when you arrive at a hotel.
B: Erm … ring the bell.
A: Erm, well, after that, after you've arrived in the room.
B: Check in? Check in?
A: No, you've arrived in the room …
B: Oh, right, in your room, erm, put your … open your bags.
A: Yes, and …
B: Unpack your clothes.
A: That's it, you unpack your luggage.

3.
A: You do this in the garden, or sometimes in the house …
B: Er, you don't dig in the house, I was going to say dig, erm, in the garden, sunbathe? You don't do that in the house either. Is it something …
A: OK, I'll give you …
B: Grow plants?
A: No, I'll give you a clue. Um, you, you pile up coal … and … or wood and you …
B: Oh, have a fire, make a fire.
A: You light a fire.
B: Light a fire, of course you do.

4.
A: You do this when you've bought something for someone.
B: Erm, keep the receipt … you've bought it for someone else, it's a present, er, you …you wrap it.
A: That's right.

5.
A: When you leave your house, you have to do this.
B: Check you've locked all the windows.
A: Nearly.
B: Erm, lock your door?
A: That's it.

6.
A: This might happen when you're doing the washing up.
B: Er, you get wet.
A: Yes, you do get wet, but you also …
B: Mmm, I always do.
A: If the water's too hot …
B: If the water's too hot, er, you might break a glass.
A: Well, no, what would happen to you?
B: Oh, erm, you'd burn yourself, you'd scald your hand or something.
A: That's it.

## 7 COURSES

### 6 Listen and answer

1. Is a loan something to do with money?
2. If you fail an exam, are you happy?
3. Can you pour a suitcase?
4. Is an acrobat a kind of performer?
5. If you mimic someone, do you sound like them?
6. Is a character a person in a play?
7. If you have a talent for something, does it mean you are hopeless at it?
8. Can you carry something on a tray?
9. Does it help a ballet dancer to be agile?
10. If you enrol for a course, does it mean you pass it?
11. Is a seminar similar to a lecture?
12. Can you order something from a waiter?
13. Is a script something you can eat?
14. Is literature a science subject?
15. If you are willing to do something, do you want to do it?

## 8 ALL IN A DAY'S WORK

### 5 Listen and answer

1. Can a dictionary solve language problems?
2. If you have a day off, do you go to work?
3. If you share something, do you keep it to yourself?
4. If you lack experience in a job, are you new to it?
5. If you work for yourself, do you pay yourself?
6. Is an advantage a good thing?
7. If you are *for* something, are you against it?
8. Is minus the opposite of plus?

9. Is a budget something to do with money?
10. Is a colleague something you can write?
11. Is a sales representative someone who buys for a company?
12. If you get sickness pay, are you healthy?

## 9 FROM THE CRADLE TO THE GRAVE

### 7 Melinda's wedding

Well, a wedding's a lot of work, I can tell you that. For ours we made lists for months before – we put people on our guest list, we crossed them out, we put them on again. We made lists of food, we asked a friend to make our cake, another to ice it. And we decided what delicious food we wanted to eat, and we asked friends to bring a dish of food on the day. Well, it's not very conventional, but we didn't have much money at the time. And an old family friend made my dress to my design – a medieval design – and I wore a garland of flowers and fruits in my hair. And my husband and his best man hired morning suits and top hats.

We spoke to the vicar about having our wedding in his beautiful church. And we arranged the choir, and lovely poems to be read. And an opera singer friend said that she would sing for us, which was wonderful. And we invited about seventy people. Um, I had one bridesmaid to hold my bouquet, and when I arrived at the altar I realised I'd left my flowers behind, and my little bridesmaid had nothing to hold, but it didn't matter – we were too happy to let it matter.

Um, the service was quite thoughtful and beautiful, and lots of people cried, so it must have been really good. Um, then we signed the register after the service, and we were married.

Then we had champagne in the vicar's garden, and had lots of speeches which was lovely. And then we walked round the corner to an old pub next to the church and had lots of lovely food. And after we'd eaten, family and friends made speeches and told embarrassing stories that made both my husband and I blush – they weren't true of course, these stories. And we drank champagne and laughed a lot, and then we cut our cake and then we left for our honeymoon. And that was two weeks in the sun before coming home, an old married couple.

## 10 PHONAHOLICS

### 1 Telephone conversations

B

1.
A: Hello?
B: Oh, hello. is that Maria?
A: No, it's Ursula. I'm afraid Maria's out at the moment.
B: Oh, right. Do you know what time she'll be back?
A: Um, later this afternoon, I think – about five o'clock.
B: I see. Well, in that case, could I leave a message?
A: Yes, of course. Hang on a minute, I'll just get a pen. OK, go ahead.
B: Right. Could you ask her to ring me when she gets back? My name is Catherine. She's got my number.
A: OK, I'll tell her as soon as she gets in.
B: Thanks very much. Bye.
A: Bye.

2.
A: Morton and Benson, Solicitors. Can I help you?
B: Yes, could I speak to Catherine Benson, please?
A: Yes, who shall I say is calling?
B: My name is Derek Silver. I'm an old client of hers.
A: Right, Mr Silver. If you'd just like to hold the line for a moment, then I'll put you through.
B: OK, thanks.

3.

A: Hello.

B: Hi, Sarah, it's James. How are you?

A: Fine. And you?

B: Yeah, I'm OK. Listen, I'm ringing about this evening. I need to ask you a big favour.

A: Oh, yes. What is it?

B: Well, I'm afraid I've got no transport. Do you think you could give me a lift to the party in your car?

A: Yeah, sure, of course.

B: Oh, great. Thanks a lot.

A: What time shall I pick you up, then?

B: Um, eight?

A: Yes, that's fine. I'll see you later, then.

B: Yes, OK. Bye.

## 6 Half a conversation

Hello? Phil, is that you?

So, how are you?

Brilliant! How did it go?

Was the birth all right? No problems?

That's good. And is the baby OK now?

Oh, it sounds wonderful. And how's Vicky? Is she all right too?

Yeah? So there weren't any problems at all?

That's wonderful. And, and does she look like you?

What – dark hair?

Oh. And have you thought of any names at all? Have you decided?

Oh, I can't wait to see her. And do you know when Vicky's coming out of hospital?

Good. Oh, wonderful, I'm so pleased. I can't wait to see you all.

OK then, bye bye.

## 11 GOODS AND SERVICES

### 4 Getting things done

C

C: Where did you have the FILM developed?

D: Oh, I sent it to a LABORATORY.

C: Were the photos GOOD?

D: Mmm, they were WONDERFUL.

E: Where are you GOING?

F: I'm going to have my EYES tested.

E: Why? Do you need GLASSES?

F: I HOPE not!

G: Oh, no, my WATCH is broken.

H: Well, you'd better have it REPAIRED.

G: Yes, but WHERE?

H: At a JEWELLER'S, I suppose.

I: My CAR has broken down again.

J: Oh, dear. What HAPPENED?

I: I forgot to have it SERVICED.

J: Well, that was SILLY, wasn't it?

### 6 Displaying the goods

As soon as you enter a shop, you will probably see different kinds of display. For example, one of the most common is a wall display, and the point or special feature of a wall is that you only see the product from the front.

An alternative is an island display. This will be a small island in the middle of the shop, and that means that a product displayed there can be seen from all sides. Islands also give special prominence to products.

Many shops also have glass counters and these can be very useful for displaying goods. You can see the product easily, but at the same time the product is under the glass and therefore safe. More and more shops now seem to have hanging displays. These may be on a rail, or suspended from a wall or the ceiling. One advantage of this method is that you can often get a lot of products in a small space.

Then of course there are refrigerators, which are obviously essential to display products which must be kept chilled or frozen.

And finally there are what's called dump bins. Basically these are large boxes full of a particular product and customers just help themselves. One advantage of dump bins is that the display doesn't need to be kept tidy, and this saves time. It's important, however, to make sure that the bin is always full – an empty dump bin is a sad sight and doesn't encourage sales.

## 12 BARE NECESSITIES

### 6 Living in basic conditions

1. Joan

I was on holiday last year in North Wales with a friend who kept hauling me out on very long walks. And one day we decided to do part of Snowdon, so we set off very equipped for our day with our walking boots and our rucksacks and everything we needed. And the weather was glorious when we set off. And midway through the afternoon the mist came in and rather than carry on and lose our way, we actually decided to stand still and see what happened. In fact, the mist became worse, it became deep fog, and so we decided to stay there for the night and we survived on a small bottle of water and two bananas. So I have never been so glad to see the sun come up and the fog disappear.

2. David

A friend of mine and I were driving out of Birmingham and there was an enormous traffic jam and we thought we were going to be there for about half an hour at least. But half an hour turned into an hour and the traffic didn't move at all – we moved about, I don't know, fifty yards in something like two and a half hours. And we got terribly, terribly hungry, and … I've never really liked sugared almonds at all, I've always – if there's a sugared almond in a chocolate box, I always leave it at the bottom or maybe even throw the box away – but there were some sugared almonds in the, in the glove compartment of the car, and after not having any food for three whole hours, I've never tasted anything more delicious in my entire life.

3. Nick

Yes, this happened when I was visiting the Isles of Scilly, a place that I often go to with my family or with friends and, um, I went to what they call an 'off' island – which is one of the islands with very few people on it – for an evening drink. And I got talking to two guys who'd come over on a yacht and, um, they said I could go back with them, which sounded great, but then the fog came in so we had to spend the night on the island. And, er, we had to stay in, er, a reading room which was just a little hut really with a stone floor. And, um, all we had to, to get us through the night were little bottles of Orangina, which is a horrible orange squash that I never really drink normally. And we had that and some crisps. And I just, I was so grateful when the sun came up and – at six o'clock the next morning – and we could sail back on this boat. It seemed like a long night.

## 13 WHO IS REALLY ON TRIAL?

### 6 How to beat car theft

Every 75 seconds a car is stolen somewhere in the UK. That's more than 425,000 a year, and of those about 100,000 are never found – most of these are cut up and sold as parts or possibly sold abroad.

In many cases we don't help matters much either – 1 in 4 of all cars stolen were left unlocked by their owners or were left with the keys in the ignition.

Now this is stupid, and there are certainly many things we can do ourselves to beat car crime:

First, you should mark the vehicle identity number in lots of different places in the car – this will make it much more difficult for a thief to sell it.

Secondly, you should park in well-lit areas and try to avoid parking in the same place every day.

Don't leave your licence or registration documents in the car. Thieves can use them to sell the car illegally.

And please don't leave valuables in the car where they can be seen – that only attracts car thieves. A portable or security coded radio is also advisable.

Finally, and very importantly, fit an alarm, but please not one that goes off when someone blows their nose three hundred metres away or when the wind blows. False alarms are very irritating, and in the end, of course, people will take no notice if they go off.

## 14 TALL STORIES, SHORT STORIES

### 6 I never forget a face (II)

So when the two of us found ourselves alone in the carriage, I started to talk, just as if we were old friends. But I can't say that I got very much information out of him. He spoke well, with a friendly manner, but he told me very little. He looked a bit tired, I remember, as if he'd been working too hard lately, and I thought maybe that made him unwilling to talk much.

Well, to cut a long story short, I had to give up. I'd told him a lot about myself, of course, so as to make things pleasant. I'd even boasted about a rather nice bit of business I'd done that morning. He seemed interested in a quiet sort of way, but it was no good, and the next time I looked at him, he'd put his head back and gone off to sleep!

We were just running into the station then and though the train stopped rather suddenly, it didn't seem to wake him. So I touched him sharply on the knee.

'Wake up, old fellow! We're there!' I said.

He awoke at once and smiled at me.

You know what the weather was like just then. When we came out of the station together, it was quite dark and raining heavily. There was a wind blowing and it was bitterly cold. I turned round and said to him:

'Listen. There isn't a bus for a quarter of an hour. I've got my car in the station-yard, and if you're in one of those small houses I can take you there.'

'Thanks very much,' he said, and off we went.

'This is very kind of you,' he said, as we started, and that was the last thing he said until we were half way across the open country.

Then he suddenly turned round and said, 'You can let me get out here.'

'What, here?' I asked him. It seemed mad, because there wasn't a house within five hundred yards. But I slowed down, as anyone would.

The next thing that happened was that something hit me terribly hard on the back of the head. I fell forwards and then everything went black. When I came to myself again, I was lying in the ditch with the rain pouring down on me, with a bad headache, no car in sight and my pockets – as I found out later – empty.

I went straight to the police station, of course. And there I reported that someone had stolen my car, a new umbrella, a gold watch and a hundred and fifty-two pounds ten shillings in notes.

Of course, as soon as I got there I remembered who the man was. His picture was on the wall outside. I'd seen it every day for a week. That's why his face reminded me of Bardfield. Under the picture were some words: 'Wanted for Robbery with Violence and Attempted Murder. John …'

Oh, dear. I've forgotten the name again. I just can't keep names in my head. But that's the man. I tell you, I never forget a face.

## 15 LOVE THY NEIGHBOUR

### 6 The Living Flag

In June 1944, a salesman from the Fisher Hat company called at a local store in Lake Wobegon and offered the owner, Herman Hochstetter, a good deal on red and blue baseball caps.

'Do you have white ones too?' Herman asked.

The salesman thought that white caps could be had for the same wonderful price. Herman ordered two hundred red, two hundred white and one hundred blue. By the end of the year, he still had four hundred and eighty caps. So the inspiration of the Living Flag was born out of that.

On June 14, 1945, a good crowd assembled in front of the Central building. His wife Louise handed out the caps, while Herman stood on a stepladder and told people where to stand. He lined up the reds and whites into stripes, then got the blues into their square. They sang the national anthem and then the Living Flag dispersed.

People were happy to do what they were told and stand in place, but in 1946 and 1947, people complained about the heat and about Herman. What gave *him* the idea he could order *them* around?

'People! Please! I need your attention! You blue people, put your hats on! Let's do this without talking! Everybody shut up! Please!'

One problem was that none of them got to see the flag they were in; the picture in the newspaper was in black and white. Only Herman saw the real flag. People wanted a chance to go up on the roof and see the spectacle for themselves.

Then on Flag Day, 1949, just as Herman said, 'That's it! Hold it now!' one of the reds made a break for it, and ran up four flights of stairs to the roof and had a long look at the flag.

'How does it look?' people shouted up to him.

'Unbelievable! I can't describe it!' he said.

So then everyone had to have a look. One by one, members of the Living Flag went up to the roof. It *was* marvellous!

It took *hours*.

## 16 YES AND NO

### 3 Agreeing with each other

B
1. I work quite hard.
2. I don't like strong coffee.
3. I can't play tennis very well.
4. I didn't enjoy the film.
5. I loved her first book.
6. I haven't seen him today.
7. I haven't got my credit card with me.
8. I don't want any salad.

## 6 Saying *no* politely

**A**

1. Would you like to come to the cinema this evening?
2. Could you possibly lend me £10 until tomorrow?
3. Would you like a lift to the station?
4. Are you going to Neema's party this evening?
5. Do you want any help tomorrow?
6. Could you drive us to the station?

**B**

1. Would you like to come to the cinema this evening?
   I'd love to, but I'm afraid I have to stay in and do some work.
2. Could you possibly lend me £10 until tomorrow?
   I wish I could, but I'm afraid I'm absolutely broke.
3. Would you like a lift to the station?
   That's very kind of you, but my dad has already offered to take me.
4. Are you going to Neema's party this evening?
   I wish I could, but I'm afraid I'm busy.
5. Do you want any help tomorrow?
   Oh, that's very kind of you to offer, but I think I can manage.
6. Could you drive us to the station?
   Oh, I'm terribly sorry, I can't. I'm afraid the car is in the garage at the moment.

## 17 PACKAGING

### 3 Building words and shifting stress

| | |
|---|---|
| power | powerful |
| simplicity | simple |
| danger | dangerous |
| mystery | mysterious |
| elegance | elegant |
| luxury | luxurious |
| glamour | glamorous |
| security | secure |
| history | historical |
| similarity | similar |

### 6 Sorry I got it wrong

During a 75-year lifetime, the average person in Britain eats:
18,270 pounds of potatoes
16,761 eggs
49,075 loaves of bread
16,341 pints of mineral water
14,571 pints of beer
716 cans of baked beans
18 pounds of dirt
8 whole cows
36 sheep
36 pigs
7500 chickens
and uses 65 miles of toilet paper

- Mississippians eat earth as a snack – you can have it smooth and sherbet like, sweet and chalky or sour and metallic.

- In 1985, a South African man was taken to hospital having just eaten 53 tubes of toothpaste, two telescopic aerials, two razors and 150 disposable razor handles.

- A psycho-neurotic 24-year-old American woman ate a five-inch iron bolt from her hospital door, which incredibly went through her intestines but broke the bed pan when she finally passed it.

- The heaviest object ever to have been extracted from a human stomach was a 5lb 3 oz ball of wool which had been eaten by a Cornish girl and was surgically removed in 1985.

- William Pitt the Younger (1759–1806) allegedly drank 574 bottles of claret, 854 bottles of Madeira and 2,400 bottles of port in one year.

- In Chicago in 1880, as part of an 'outrageous' contest, Jay Gwaltney, then aged 19, managed to munch his way through an 11-foot birch tree in 85 hours.

## 18 HONESTLY SPEAKING

### 6 Honestly!

SPEAKER 1

Um, I went to a friend's for supper the other night and, um, she'd cooked a vegetarian lasagne on the assumption that I was a vegetarian, which in fact I'm not, and I've never been. Um, but I lied because she'd gone to all this trouble and I said, 'Yes, yes, of course I'm a vegetarian; that's, that's very, that's great, you know, lovely'. And we sat down to this meal which was utterly disgusting; I wanted to vomit at every mouthful. But, um, she kept asking me had I done it right, and you know she'd followed this recipe, so I kept saying 'Yes, it's great, lovely', and I had to finish the whole thing. Ugh!

SPEAKER 2

Well it was about last year. I was supposed to be revising for my exams, and I asked my mum if I could go round to my friend's house to revise. And she said 'OK', so I went round to my friend's house but of course we didn't really want to revise. So we decided to go to the cinema. So we went and got in to see the film, which was really boring and a complete waste of time, and as luck would have it, as we came out of the cinema who was there but my mum who'd decided to go and see the same film with my aunt. And so of course she saw me and she never let me go to my friend's house again to revise.

SPEAKER 3

This was shortly before we got married and we went to my mother-in-law's house and there was a very strange new object in the house. It was a ... it didn't fit in with anything there. It was a lamp, which the base of it was a parrot and the top of it was a very large lampshade covered with parrots. And it was so extraordinary that we looked at each other and then we both felt we had to say what a lovely lamp it was even though we really meant what a completely extraordinary thing it was. And she said, 'I'm so glad you like it because I'm giving it to you for your wedding present'. So we said, 'Oh, lovely', but of course we didn't really want it at all, we said there wasn't room in the car to collect it just then, and we kept not collecting it, and finally we did collect it and of course when she came to visit it had to be displayed in the living room.

## 19 PLAIN ENGLISH

### 5 Word stress, sentence stress

1. It was only a small advertisement but two hundred people applied for the job.
2. The government's educational policy is excellent for children between the ages of 4 and 6.
3. I've been unemployed since I lost my job last year.
4. Our company isn't doing very well, so the management have invited a firm of consultants to give us some advice.
5. The company specialises in computer software.
6. Some politicians have no idea how to govern the country.
7. The factory employs about 150 workers.
8. It was really embarrassing when the interviewer asked me about my previous job. I knew he didn't think I was a serious applicant for the post.

## 7 My mind went completely blank

SPEAKER 1

I was doing a writing class, and we had to write a short story, and then read it out loud. When it was my turn I was so scared. I felt, oh, just so nervous, not about reading it out loud but because it was something I had written. So I, I started to read and my voice started to shake, and I blushed, oh, it was terrible. But I made it to the end, and everyone was really nice about the story, so it wasn't so bad.

SPEAKER 2

Um, I was walking back from the tube one night and … not something I do very often … and I was aware of footsteps behind me and I didn't dare turn around. And I started to walk faster and faster, and the steps seemed to follow me. And my, my mind went blank. I started to go the wrong way home … I went down a side street I never go down, and I was shaking … and, and my hands were sweating and my mouth went dry. I just didn't know what was happening. And I panicked so much that I just, I just walked up to the first front door where there was a light on and rang the bell. And fortunately somebody answered the door and I asked if I could use their telephone. And, um, it was, er, a woman behind me with an umbrella all the time.

SPEAKER 3

My little sister had a baby recently, and she asked me to be the godmother and to say a few words at the, um, at the christening. And the night before this I wasn't nervous at all, I thought it'd be fine. But when it actually came to it, I stood up, and I could see all our family there, and all our friends and everybody, and suddenly I could feel myself getting nervous. I started to shake. And at the crucial point my mind went completely blank, and I forgot the baby's name and thanked everybody for coming to the funeral.

## 20 ART AND SOCIETY

### 6 I know what I like

1. *Le bain*
1. Tony: Two things struck me immediately about this picture. One … the first thing was that this woman has some clothes on in this bath – I was wondering why. And the second thing was that it seems to be principally kind of made up of different hues of blue, that I actually quite like.
2. Ian: I like this painting a lot. This … the colours are my kind of colours, um, blues, different shades of blues. I like the subject, the lady in the bath with the flowers. Er, my kind of painting.
3. Patience: It's a very restful painting. She looks as though she's very relaxed, and she's holding some lovely flowers in her hand and looking into space and thinking beautiful thoughts.
4. Julia: I don't really like that painting very much. Um, I don't know, there seems to be … maybe there's a story behind it or something like that, but no, it's not my kind of painting at all. I don't really like it.

2. *Le vase bleu*
1. Tony: Now this one I don't like at all. I'm not very keen on flowers and fruit and things and vases. All seems a bit boring to me.
2. Ian: This is a lovely painting, a beautiful painting. Lovely colours, very subtle, very soft, flowers, I think fruit in the foreground. Um, a very relaxing, soft, gentle painting.
3. Patience: It's not a painting I'd really want in my house. It's all right, but I've seen better.
4. Julia: Well, I quite like this painting. I mean, I think it would look nice in, um, in a kitchen, or something, because it's quite, it's quite colourful, and it's quite pretty and, um, be nice in your house, but … it's nothing special particularly.

3. *Au café*
1. Tony: I actually quite like this picture. It's, uh … it seems to … to … inspire some feeling. Uh, you know, there's an emotional response to this picture, I think about loneliness and despair. Yeah, I like it.
2. Ian: Er, this is one of the most awful paintings I've ever seen. It was obviously painted by a complete amateur. The colours are ghastly, um, the shades are wrong. Um, I don't know who painted this painting, but I would pay a lot of money not to have it anywhere near me.
3. Patience: Yes, it's got, er, atmosphere this painting. Those two people, they've probably sat next to each other, year in year out, in that pub, or winebar or whatever it is. And they've run out of things to say to each other, so they're just sitting, lost in thought.
4. Julia: Oh, I love that picture, that is really lovely. Look at her face. That's my kind of picture, 'cause um, it just makes you wonder what she's thinking about. Yeah, I really like that.

## 21 DARE YOURSELF TO SUCCEED

### 4 Weak forms and linking

1. I could've left the company sooner if I'd heard about the other job.
2. He'd have regretted it if he'd thrown it away.
3. We might never have bought the flat if we'd known about the water problem.
4. If Janet had seen you, she would've been thrilled.
5. If we hadn't got there at 6 o'clock, we'd've had to catch the next boat.
6. The president wouldn't have won the election if the newspapers hadn't supported him.

### 6 Different lives

SPEAKER 1

I was brought up in a city and, uh, so I never really had anything to do with horses, except to see them when policemen rode them along the streets until a friend of mine who used to go riding regularly rang up – and her car had broken down – and she asked me if I could give her a lift to her riding school, which I did. And she persuaded me to have a riding lesson, which was lovely. We went across some fields and on the road. It was very gentle, nothing very frightening – and I was hooked. And from that on, I used to go to riding lessons every week, and I got completely addicted and became rather good, and have been to some gymkhanas and won myself some rosettes, and I think now if my friend's car hadn't broken down, I would never have learned to ride.

SPEAKER 2

Some years ago now I bought my first flat and I'd arranged with a local builder and decorator to come round and decorate the whole place for me. Well, on the night before he was due to arrive, he rang me up and apologised and said he had fallen off his ladder and broken his leg and he couldn't possibly do the job. Well, I was very fed up living in this rather squalid flat with flaking ceilings and mouldy wallpaper, that I decided I'd do it all myself. And I did. Next day I went out and bought all the equipment and, and a book to tell me how to do it, and I set to and did it. And it was great. I found it very easy and extremely enjoyable. I could even hang wallpaper, even ceiling paper, it was great. Well, I enjoyed it so much that I started to do it for friends, and then people started paying me for doing it. And now several flats later, I've got a thriving little business on the side, and that wouldn't have happened if that poor man hadn't fallen off his ladder and broken his leg.

## 22 FORCES OF NATURE

### 4 Text reading

It was midnight on 8 February, 1971. The children were in bed but I couldn't sleep, so I opened the front door and stood looking out at the beautiful evening. There was a black sky and a full moon, but it was unusually quiet. Normally there were hundreds of animals moving about – snakes, lizards, squirrels – but they'd all gone. I'm absolutely convinced they knew something was going to happen.

### 6 I couldn't get used to that

SPEAKER 1

Well, it's a very simple and, er, obvious thing, um, that I found very difficult to get used to as an English person, British person, is driving on the right side of the road – to the extent that when we left the ferry very early one morning, having arrived in France, I literally nearly killed my whole family by turning the wrong way, um, as we, as we left, uh, the port.

SPEAKER 2

One of the best holidays I had was in Athens with a friend of mine who lives there now. And it was fantastic, it's such a beautiful place. But the thing I couldn't get used to was the heat, because the sun is so hot there, and Athens is, um, situated in sort of like a bowl between all these, um, hills, and the pollution is terrible and I just couldn't get used to that.

SPEAKER 3

The one thing I can never get used to when I go abroad is the currency. The coins are all different sizes and they're all different shapes and weights, and I can never get used to them. I can never get used to how much they, how much they're worth, so I end up giving away … I'm sure I end up giving away a lot more money than I mean to.

# ANSWER KEY

## 1 LOOKING BACK AND LOOKING FORWARD

### 1 Words with similar meanings

**A**

great – terrific
scared stiff – terrified
upset – unhappy
worried – anxious
relaxed – calm
nervous – tense
awful – dreadful
boring – dull
huge – enormous

**B**

*Possible answers:*
1. Yes, I'm quite tense.
2. Yes, I was terrified.
3. Yes, it's dreadful.
4. Yes, he did look anxious.
5. Yes, she's still upset about it.
6. Yes, they make me relaxed.
7. Yes, it was terrific.
8. Yes, he was very boring.

### 2 Something's missing here

**A**

heard   found   saw   bought   threw   hurt
caught/taught   wore/tore   lost/cost   chose
knew   sent/bent/lent/went   hit/bit   slept
won   spent   flew/blew   told/sold

**B**

1. He (or we) sent two parcels to his brother for his birthday.
2. The plane flew very low over our heads.
3. My teacher taught me everything I know.
4. Last week you told me your sister was ill.
5. The dinner cost more than she had.
6. The team won the football match, but lost the cup.

### 3 Grouping words by topic

Transport: van, season ticket, parking space
Accommodation: bed and breakfast, cottage, bungalow
Finance: loan, bill, credit card
Leisure: gardening, drawing, sunbathing
Possessions : jewellery, wallet, diary
Health and fitness: diet, weight training, tracksuit

### 4 Word stress in compounds

traffic jam   primary school   central heating
zebra crossing   false teeth   income tax
air conditioning   post office   parking meter
credit card   car park   washing machine
compact disc

### 5 Famous people look back

1. Michael J Fox
2. Margot Fonteyn
3. Jackie Joyner-Kersee
4. Jackie Joyner-Kersee
5. Margot Fonteyn
6. Michael J Fox

### 6 Looking back: recent history

See tapescript for answers.

### 7 Mixed tenses

are moving; is/will be; know; started; didn't see / didn't find; saw/found; live / are living; think; will enjoy; is trying; am packing; are having

### 9 Visual dictionary

1. postbox   2. road junction / crossroads
3. traffic warden   4. litter bin   5. road sign
6. car overtaking   7. dustmen   8. roundabout
9. van   10. parking meter   11. zebra crossing
12. traffic lights   13. pavement   14. ambulance
15. pedestrian   16. number plate
17. streetlight/streetlamp   18. sports car

## 2 HOW DOES THAT SOUND?

### 1 *Hair* or *hairs*

1. correct
2. I need (*some*) clean paper to write on. (*Or* I need a clean *piece of* paper to write on.)
3. She's doing some medical *research* at the moment.
4. correct
5. I didn't think much of their *advice*, did you?
6. Have you brought all the sports *equipment*?
7. correct
8. correct
9. Have you got any previous *experience* of selling washing machines, Mr Turville?
10. correct
11. We need some more *information* about that.
12. She owns a small shop which sells antique *furniture*.

### 2 Much more interesting than I thought

*Possible answers:*
1. Gold is far more valuable than silver.
2. Fishing is much more popular than athletics.
3. Boxing is the most violent sport in the world.
4. Girls are much cleverer than boys.
5. Pronunciation is a bit more difficult than grammar.
6. The Nile is the longest river in the world.
7. The North Pole is a bit colder than the South Pole.

8. Writing by hand is much slower than typing.
9. Food is the most important thing in my life.
10. Photographs are far more interesting than drawings.

## 3 Opposites

1. The smallest city
2. The safest place
3. The worst singer
4. The oldest person
5. The ugliest view
6. The most careful drivers
7. The worst actor
8. The tallest man
9. The longest river
10. The easiest question
11. The most generous person
12. The cleverest / most intelligent student
13. The darkest room
14. The heaviest suitcase
15. The tamest animal (most domesticated)
16. The weakest coffee
17. The mildest cigarettes
18. The nicest person
19. The least competitive group
20. The least

## 4 In a soft voice

1. clearly; quickly
2. loud
3. distinctive; easily
4. irritating
5. deep
6. reassuring
7. cheerfully
8. quietly
9. reliable

## 5 Weak forms

Japan    machine    certificate    professor    reliable
career    comfortable    photographer    Arabic
weather    Italy    accommodation

## 6 Hearing dogs for the deaf

**B**
The text mentions situations 1, 2, 3, 5 and 6.

**C**
'although some are donated by breeders' should go after
'rescue centres'.
'and like all hearing dogs, she's very nosy' should go
after 'when there's someone at the door'.
'(the same model as that belonging to the dog's future
owner)' should go after 'alarm clocks'.
'that most people who can hear never even think about'
should go after 'sounds' and before 'such as'.

## 7 Where would you hear it?

| Where | Message |
|---|---|
| 1. On a train | The train is arriving at Kings Cross station. |
| 2. In a department store | The message tells customers about special reductions and about a fashion show at 11.30. |
| 3. In a plane | The plane is landing at Gatwick Airport soon. Passengers should fasten seat belts and shouldn't smoke. |
| 4. Airport | A security alert. Instructions on what to do. |
| 5. Art gallery | The gallery is closing in five minutes. The gift shop stays open another half hour. The gallery opens at 9am the next day. |

## 8 Sound story

*Possible answer:*
Suddenly I heard the sound of a dog barking at the front
door. I got up from my chair and went to have a look.
When I opened the door I saw the dog and it started
barking even louder. 'What is it?' I said. 'What's wrong?'
The dog turned and began to run off, so I followed. In
the distance I could hear a voice crying for help.
Eventually the dog took me to where a man was lying
on the ground. 'What happened? Are you OK?' I asked.
The man could hardly speak and was obviously badly
injured, so I ran back to the house, and called for the
police and an ambulance. I returned to the injured man
and soon heard the siren of an ambulance as it arrived.
The dog was by my side panting. 'Good girl, well done,'
I said.

## 10 Visual dictionary

**kitchen equipment** (U):    1. tin opener (C)
2. food mixer (C)    3. bottle opener (C)
4. saucepan (C)    5. frying pan (C)    6. toaster (C)
**furniture** (U):    7. coffee table (C)    8. sofabed (C)
9. chest of drawers (C)    10. stool (C)
**luggage** (U):    11. rucksack/backpack (C)
12. briefcase (C)    13. suitcase (C)
14. shoulder bag (C)
**paper** (U):    15. writing paper (U)    16. tissues (C)
17. toilet paper (U)    18. wrapping paper (U)
19. newspaper (C)
**transport** (U):    20. lorry (C)    21. motorbike (C)
22. coach (C)    23. bicycle (C)

## 3 GAMES PEOPLE PLAY

## 1 What are you talking about?

A:  spending; to accept; to play; trying
     The text is about golf.
B:  doing; to be; to do *or* doing (both are correct);
     getting up
     The text is about athletics: running marathon, for
     example.

C: playing; watching; playing; to take; to persuade; to buy

The text is about chess.

## 2 Are you good at sport?

1. good at; interested in
2. afraid of
3. worried about
4. proud of
5. depends on
6. shy about
7. fear of
8. kind of
9. point of

## 3 A wall of sound

1. It's a kind of animal.
2. You need a lot of skill.
3. The rules are difficult at first.
4. I got it from a shop in Athens.
5. I'm optimistic about the future.
6. She didn't win anything at all.
7. He gave it up at the end of last week.
8. I'm not worried about it at the moment.

## 4 Full of skill or skilful?

**A**

Nouns: boredom; confidence; skill; competition; interest; shyness; fear; optimism; knowledge

**B**

2. Sue is shy.
3. Mark is knowledgeable.
4. Jane is competitive.
5. Marta is optimistic.
6. Lino has (a lot of) confidence.
7. Alana suffers from boredom.
8. Julian has a lot of skill.

## 5 Women are catching up

1. Women do more sport than they used to; they are more dedicated and competitive; the technology is better.
2. Men tend to be bigger and stronger; they have better hearts and lungs; they take part in sport more.
3. b

## 6 What does that mean?

*Possible answers:*
1. It means the same as *hate*. (*Or* It's the opposite of *love*.)
2. It's a place where people gamble / win or lose money / you can play roulette and other games for money.
3. It's someone who takes part in a game show.
4. It's someone who controls a sports match or game.
5. It's where you run or race in an athletics meeting.
6. It means the same as *frightened*.
7. It's a kind of staircase that you can move.
8. It's a thing you use for hitting a ball.
9. It's the stuff you use to clean your teeth.

## 8 Visual dictionary

1. sports shirt   2. shorts   3. tracksuit
4. football boots   5. helmet   6. saddle   7. skates
8. trainers   9. saddle   10. helmet
11. tennis racquet   12. hockey stick   13. baseball bat
14. golf clubs   15. board game   16. chess pieces
17. counters   18. dice   19. trunks   20. goggles
21. swimming costume   22. fishing rod
23. fishing net   24. stopwatch   25. javelin
26. hurdle

## 4 NEWSPAPERS AND MAGAZINES

## 1 How long?

1. How long did you have it?
2. How long have you lived with her?
3. How long have you had it?
4. How long have you known him?
5. How long did it last? / How long did you stay there?
6. How long have you worn/had them?
7. How long did you have it?
8. How long have you been a vegetarian?

## 2 The press in Britain

1. broadsheets   2. tabloid newspapers
3. circulation figures   4/5. journalists/reporters
6. scoop   7. Headlines   8. print   9. articles
10/11. international news/home news   12. copies
13. editors

## 3 Grouping words by topic

magazine and newspaper publishing: circulation subscription   scandal   editor   article   column
medicine: cancer   illness   drugs   treatment suffer   diagnose
business: company   revenue   sales   profit shareholder   invest

## 4 When and where?

1. in   2. by   3. At   4. during   5. since   6. at
7. for   8. in   9. on   10. in   11. at/on   12. for
13. at

## 5 Women & Guns

1. She was worried about security in her jewellery business.
2. By subscription only.
3. 12 million.
4. Yes, it does.
5. Because they are worried that they might kill their husbands.
6. You can see a gun carried at the ankle if the dress isn't long enough.

## 6 What do you read?

|  | What do they read? | Why? |
|---|---|---|
| Speaker 1 | Reader's Digest | She likes positive stories. |
|  | Marie Claire | Because of the fashion, cooking and cosmetic adverts. |
| Speaker 2 | Elle/Cosmopolitan | No reason given. |
|  | Marie Claire | It has good features; not too many adverts; she likes horoscopes and fashion. |
|  | Time Out | Because it tells you what's happening in London (cinema, exhibitions, etc.). |
| Speaker 3 | Body Builder | He's getting into shape, and it gives tips on fashions and techniques. |
| Speaker 4 | Time Out | For the cinema and theatre information and reviews and the comment and editorials. |
|  | Hello! | It's good for waiting rooms. |

## 5 RELATIONSHIPS

### 1 Who's your father-in-law?

1. T
2. F (She is your sister-in-law.)
3. F (He would be your stepbrother.)
4. T
5. F (They are the children of your aunts and uncles.)
6. T
7. T
8. F (They are relatives or relations. Your mother and father are your parents.)
9. T
10. F (You can.)

### 2 *Ships* and *hoods*

**A**

-*ship*: partnership, relationship, leadership, dictatorship, membership, apprenticeship

-*hood*: fatherhood, parenthood, adulthood, childhood

**B**

1. partnership   2. Adulthood   3. apprenticeship
4. Parenthood/Fatherhood   5. Leadership
6. dictatorship   7. relationship   8. Membership

## 5 I was the youngest

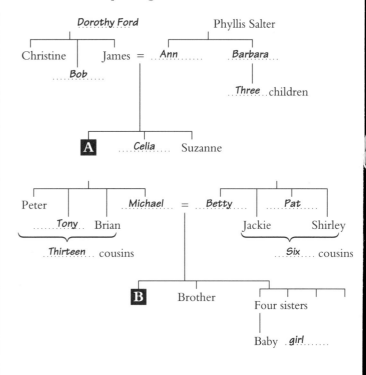

## 6 Love-hate relationships

**A**

The two couples are A and C, and B and D.
A is Dan, B is Jane, C is Jill, D is Alex.

**B**

fortunate: unlucky
to ignore: to pay attention
to wake up: to fall asleep
ugly: good-looking
modest: arrogant
married: divorced, separated
to look forward to something: to dread
badly-educated: well-educated

## 7 Reference words

**A**

1. their   2. them   3. that   4. these   5. there
6. which   7. who

**B**

1. His   2. who   3. his   4. His/Their   5. he
6. which   7. his   8. his   9. these   10. them
11. their

## 9 Visual dictionary

Work relationships: colleague; assistant; boss; supervisor; partner; client

Friendly relationships: flatmate; fiancé(e); classmate; neighbour; acquaintance; partner

Family relationships: cousin; granny; niece; stepsister; relatives; daughter-in-law; mum

The two words only used informally are *granny* and *mum*.

## 6 LIFE'S LITTLE CHORES

### 1 Diary extract

was having; rang; asked; ate; ran; was standing; gave; hurried; was sitting; was; knew; was; said; went; was lying; said; interrupted; said; replied

### 2 Plug in a TV

light a fire
get off a bus
spill coffee
pack a suitcase
wrap up a present
fasten a seat belt
go out with friends
jump a queue
do up a jacket
fold my arms
hurt my foot

### 3 Can you do it to yourself?

1. got bitten
2. cut himself
3. burnt herself
4. enjoyed themselves
5. got mugged
6. got run over
7. look after ourselves
8. scalded herself
9. got injured
10. introduced herself

### 4 Odd one out

1. elbow    2. hurry    3. fasten    4. suppose
5. supermarket

### 5 Another ordinary day

*Possible answer:*
8.40am
It was a miserable day but I decided to **go out** and spend some money. I had breakfast and then went to my local bank. The cashier wasn't very **helpful** but I cashed ~~him~~ a cheque and then I set off for town. On the way someone stopped me and said he was looking for the nearest bank. I told him **where it was**, and he thanked me and walked off in the opposite direction.

It was now ten o'clock and the roads were getting quite **busy.** I met an old friend who asked me for the money **I** owed **him**. I told him I was in a hurry and I walked off **quickly** to find a taxi.

I went into a coffee bar. It was almost **empty** except for one table where a young couple were obviously having a very intimate conversation.

Later I found myself on a street corner next to an old lady. Suddenly, out of nowhere, a youth came running down the street, grabbed her bag and **ran** away. A man on the opposite side of the street saw **what happened** and shouted for help. I ran to the nearest phone box and rang the police. By now it was pouring with rain and I decided to go home. I saw a bus coming down the street, so I pushed my way to the **front** of the queue and got **on.**

When I got home I **unlocked** the front door and went in. I was feeling quite tired and I **got undressed and** fell asleep on the sofa.

### 6 Guess what she's talking about

**B**
1. fasten your seat belt    2. unpack your luggage
3. light a fire    4. wrap it up    5. lock the door
6. burn yourself

### 7 Please *do* something!

Dear Sir or Madam,
I have had a current account with your bank for over twenty years, and have used your branch for the last two years, since I moved to Mornington.

I have now reached the point where I can no longer tolerate the queues in your branch. I have tried going to the bank at different times of the day; undoubtedly lunchtime is the worst time, but I never seem to get served without a wait of at least ten minutes. I think there are two reasons for this. Firstly, the branch appears seriously understaffed relative to the number of customers. If this is the case, you clearly need to employ more people. And secondly, each counter position has a separate queue. It would make much more sense to have a single queue, and for people to go to a counter as soon as one becomes free. This is common practice in most branches these days, so I am surprised that it is not used in your branch.

I look forward to hearing from you on this matter.
Yours faithfully,

## 7 COURSES

### 1 I studied maths and chemistry

1. correct    2. physical exercise    3. correct
4. economic    5. electronic    6. art    7. correct
8. correct    9. medicine    10. correct

### 2 The person I most admire

1. who or that    2. that or nothing
3. that or nothing    4. who, that or nothing    5. that
6. that    7. who, that or nothing    8. that or nothing

### 3 Please don't tell me what to do!

1. A: She told him to go with her.
   B: He asked her to wait a moment.
2. A: He asked her to put the TV on.
   B: She told him to do it himself.
3. A: She told her to move her car.
   B: She asked her not to give her a ticket.
4. A: She asked him to book a table for that evening.
   B: He told her not to be late.
5. A: She told him not to forget the shopping.
   B: He told her to write him a list.

### 7 Back on course

bricklaying (practical, using your hands)
watercolour painting (art)
the stock market (improving your mind)
ecology and technology (improving your mind)
glass engraving (practical, using your hands)
singing for the tone deaf (music)

drawing and painting (art)
walking in a sacred manner (improving your mind)
cookery (practical, using your hands)
shoemaking (practical, using your hands)
zero balancing – body energy with body structure (improving your mind)
karaoke singing (music)
change your life (improving your mind)
living with more meaning (improving your mind)
write your life story (improving your mind)
boomerang flying (practical, using your hands)

## 9 Visual dictionary

1. art (paintbrush, tube of paint)
2. maths (calculator, set square)
3. medicine (syringe, stethoscope)
4. geography (map, globe)
5. athletics (discus, running shoes/spikes)
6. archaeology (skull, pottery, ancient tools)
7. foreign languages (headphones, dictionary)
8. chemistry (bunsen burner, test tube)
9. music (violin, clarinet)
10. economics (graph)
11. electronics (microchip, circuit board)
12. dentistry (dentist's drill, false teeth)

# 8 ALL IN A DAY'S WORK

## 1 Do you think you could ...?

A: Hello?
B: Is that Damien Lewis?
A: Speaking.
B: **It's Carol Robins here**, Mr Lewis.
A: Hello, Carol, how can I help you?
B: Well, **I'd** very much like to come and see you this week.
A: I'm afraid that's impossible. You see, I'm going away tomorrow for a few days.
B: OK, well, perhaps I can make an appointment with you for next week then?
A: Fine. How about Tuesday at 10.00?
B: I'm very sorry but I'm **busy** at 10.00. Would it be all right **if I came** at 11.00?
A: That's fine. I'd be grateful if you could tell my secretary.
B: Sure. Many thanks.

A: (*Opening the front door*) Hello, Harry. Come in!
B: Thanks, Colin. Look, er, I wonder if **I** could borrow your ladder. We've got a problem with the roof and …
A: Oh, I'm afraid ~~but~~ that's a bit difficult. Well, in fact, impossible. Someone has stolen it.
B: Oh, no. I am sorry.
A: Actually, would it be possible **for you to** take me to the police station to report it? My car's broken down.
B: Of course. Do you mind **if** I stop at the post office on the way?
A: No, that's fine.
B: Right. Let's go, then.

## 2 It's in black and white

1. Mr and Mrs    2. neat and tidy
3. advantages and disadvantages    4. supply and demand
5. profit and loss    6. ups and downs
7. black and white    8. right and wrong

## 3 Pros and cons, good and bad

*Possible answers:*
1. to take/follow them
2. a profit
3. unpaid
4. share them
5. work for someone else
6. have it
7. against it
8. disagree
9. a disadvantage
10. make one

## 4 Putting it nicely

*Possible answers:*
1. Would it be all right if I took the afternoon off?
2. I'm very sorry, but you can't go on that training course.
3. I'd be grateful if you could shut the door on your way out.
4. I'm afraid it's out of the question for you to leave early this afternoon.
5. Do you think you could take this to the accounts office?
6. Would it be possible for you to send me the documents as soon as possible?
7. Do you mind if I close the window?
8. I wonder if you could lend me £5.

## 7 Dear Sir/Mrs Lewis/Bunty

**A**
1. Situation 3
2. The first is probably more suitable. It is less direct, more polite and a bit more formal than the second one.
3. *Would it be possible for you to …* and *Would it be all right if I …*

# 9 FROM THE CRADLE TO THE GRAVE

## 1 Sentence transformations

1. The bride and groom are given money.
2. The cars are exported to Europe.
3. The man was taken to hospital.
4. The books were sent last week.
5. The play is performed every year.
6. The film was directed by Kurosawa.
7. The man was arrested outside the theatre.
8. These sweets are made in Turkey.

## 2 Countries and nationalities

| Cities (vertical) | Countries | Nationality |
|---|---|---|
| Bucharest | Romania | Romanian |
| Prague | The Czech Republic | Czech |
| Vienna | Austria | Austrian |
| Caracas | Venezuela | Venezuelan |
| Stockholm | Sweden | Swedish |
| Helsinki | Finland | Finnish |
| Riyadh | Saudi Arabia | Saudi Arabian |
| Oslo | Norway | Norwegian |
| Istanbul | Turkey | Turkish |

| Cities (horizontal) | Countries | Nationalities |
|---|---|---|
| Athens | Greece | Greek |
| Cairo | Egypt | Egyptian |
| Seoul | South Korea | Korean |
| Milan | Italy | Italian |

## 3 Birth, marriage and death

1. bride; groom
2. ceremony; priest
3. honeymoon
4. born; baptised
5. birth; pregnant
6. funeral
7. buried
8. will

## 4 You are obliged to

1. When you enter a foreign country, you *are usually* obliged to show a passport or other form of identification.
2. You *don't have to* wear a crash helmet in a car.
3. You aren't allowed *to* use someone else's passport as if it was yours.
4. correct
5. In some Arab countries, you cannot *buy* or consume alcohol.
6. In most countries parents *are obliged* to educate their children.
7. If you travel to certain parts of the world, you *aren't supposed to* take fresh food through customs without declaring it.
8. In most countries, you *must have* (or *have to have*) a licence if you own a gun.

## 5 Same or different?

1. different   2. different   3. same   4. same
5. different   6. different   7. same   8. different

## 7 Melinda's wedding

1. true   2. true   3. false   4. true   5. true
6. false   7. true   8. true   9. false   10. true

## 10 Visual dictionary

1. choir   2. altar   3. priest   4. groom
5. best man   6. bouquet   7. aisle   8. bride
9. veil   10. bridesmaid   11. graveyard
12. gravestone   13. mourners   14. coffin
15. wreath   16. grave

## 10 PHONAHOLICS

### 1 Telephone conversations

See tapescript for possible answers.

### 2 It used to be Carthage

Zaire used to be Belgian Congo.
Thailand used to be Siam.
St Petersburg used to be Leningrad.
Slovakia used to be part of Czechoslovakia.
Ghana used to be The Gold Coast.
Estonia used to be part of the USSR.
Iran used to be Persia.
Istanbul used to be Constantinople.
Sri Lanka used to be Ceylon.
Zimbabwe used to be Rhodesia.

### 3 Cheque book and book shop

1. answerphone, phone number
2. burglar alarm, alarm call
3. telephone directory, directory enquiries
4. fax machine, machine gun
5. phone box, box office
6. marketing department, department store
7. extension number, number plate
8. lunchtime, timetable
9. physical exercise, exercise book

### 4 Harmless inventions

| Adjective | Noun | Verb | Noun |
|---|---|---|---|
| hostile | hostility | invent | invention |
| aggressive | aggression | refuse | refusal |
| safe | safety | destroy | destruction |
| violent | violence | install | installation |
| harmless | harm | accept | acceptance |
| friendly | friend(ship) | deteriorate | deterioration |

### 5 Making excuses on the phone

1. at his desk
2. wants to speak to you
3. just stepped out of the room
4. still at lunch
5. in a meeting
6. doesn't want to speak to you
7. going to be tied up all day
8. Go away

### 6 Half a conversation
**A**
A woman is ringing a man called Phil. They are friends, or she may be his sister or sister-in-law. She is calling to find out about the birth of his baby.

**B**

*Possible answers:*
Hello? Phil, is that you?
*Yes, hello!*
So, how are you?
*Well, we've had a baby girl.*
Brilliant! How did it go?
*It went very well.*
Was the birth all right? No problems?
*No, everything was fine.*
That's good. And is the baby OK now?
*She's doing really well and she's beautiful.*
Oh, it sounds wonderful. And how is Vicky? Is she all
    right too?
*Yes, fine; she's a bit tired though.*
Yeah? So there weren't any problems at all?
*No, none at all.*
That's wonderful. And does she look like you?
*No, she looks more like Vicky.*
What – dark hair?          ,
*Yes, that's right.*
Oh, and have you thought of any names at all? Have you
    decided?
*We're going to call her Rachel, I think.*
Oh, I can't wait to see her. And do you know when
    Vicky is coming out of hospital?
*She should be out on Friday.*
Good. Oh, wonderful, I'm so pleased. I can't wait to see
    you all.
*Thanks for ringing – I'll tell Vicky you rang.*
OK, then, bye bye.

## 7 Don't forget to call the office

**B**

*Possible answers:*
1. Peter,
   I had to go home for an emergency. Please cancel my
   afternoon appointments.
2. Simon,
   Your sister rang. Please ring her at her office before 6
   pm.
3. Paul,
   Max rang. He needs his books this evening and he
   sounded angry. Please do something.

## 11 GOODS AND SERVICES

### 1 If you don't keep the receipt ...

**A**
1. h    2. e    3. d    4. b    5. f    6. c    7. g    8. a

**B**

*Possible answers:*
1. you might be sorry later.
2. you'll forget it.
3. the neighbours will complain.
4. they may charge extra.
5. it will cost about £5.
6. you'll regret it.
7. you'll be able to carry it around with you.
8. they might still sell it to you.

## 2 Words ending -able or -ible

**A**
1. washable    2. breakable    3. inflatable
4. adjustable    5. unreliable    6. disposable    7. edible
8. portable    9. reversible    10. illegible

**B**

*Possible answers:*
2. glass    3. a rubber dinghy    4. a watch strap
5. a watch    6. a razor    7. a banana    8. a TV
9. a jacket    10. a letter

## 3 Product features

| Product | Features |
|---|---|
| raincoat | showerproof |
| frying pan | non-stick |
| beer | low alcohol |
| trousers | dry clean only |
| fizzy drink | low calorie |
| orange juice | no additives |
| watch | shock-resistant |
| eggs | free-range |
| tissues | extra strong |

## 4 Getting things done

See tapescript on page 134 for possible answers.

## 5 Legal rights

1. Promise 3 (not as described)
2. Promise 2 (not of proper quality)
3. Promise 2 (not of proper quality)
4. Promise 1 (not fit for normal use)
5. Promise 4 (the sales talk was not true)
6. Promise 2 (not of proper quality)

## 6 Displaying the goods

| Type of display | Special feature(s) |
|---|---|
| 1. wall display | You can only see the product from the front. |
| 2. island display | The product can be seen from all sides, and is given special prominence. |
| 3. glass counters | The product can be easily seen, but is safe. |
| 4. hanging displays | You can get a lot of products in a small space. |
| 5. refrigerators | These are essential for products which must be kept chilled or frozen. |
| 6. dump bins | The display doesn't need to be kept tidy. |

## 7 A letter of complaint

14 **W**impole **S**treet
London WC1
20 **J**anuary, 1996

Dear **Mr R**obertson,

Last **Wednesday I received** a pair of **R**obertson's **reversible** trousers from your company by mail order.

**T**he parcel was damaged on arrival and the trousers were torn. They **were** also not the **colour I** ordered.

**I** would be **grateful** if you could replace them with a blue/grey pair, and refund the postage.

**Y**ours **sincerely**,

**J**ack **E**llis

## 9 Visual dictionary

1. light bulb    2. torch    3. batteries    4. speakers
5. plug    6. electric razor    7. lead    8. computer disks    9. socket    10. tie    11. suit    12. scarf
13. gloves    14. tights    15. skirt    16. purse
17. earrings    18. cardigan    19. necklace
20. brooch    21. waistcoat    22. bracelet    23. socks

## 12 BARE NECESSITIES

### 1 Frequency and degree

1. absolutely    2. rarely / hardly ever
3. absolutely/completely    4. regularly
5. nearly/almost    6. very/really
7. Occasionally/Sometimes    8. rarely
9. extremely/very    10. regularly

### 2 Absolutely

*Possible answers:*
1. freezing/boiling
2. delicious
3. furious
4. unbelievable/incredible/astonishing
5. vital/essential/crucial
6. awful/dreadful/terrible
7. useless/hopeless
8. huge/enormous/massive (could also be fantastic/wonderful, etc.)
9. delicious/wonderful
10. tiny/minute

### 3 Dental floss and dental surgeon

1. earplug; earache    2. sleeping bag; sleeping pill
3. nail file; nail varnish    4. haircut; hairdrier
5. lampshade; lamp-post    6. spare room; spare tyre
7. toothpick; toothache    8. shoehorn; shoelace

### 4 My heart beats

1. beats    2. boil    3. landed    4. melts    5. burn
6. throw away / throw out / get rid of
7. swap/change    8. keep    9. heat    10. measured

## 5 Handbag secrets

Words in the text that mean *strange* are:
*wacky, odd(est), weird(est), unusual.*
2. They carry things in their bag for sentimental reasons, e.g. the toe from the dog's rubber toy. This reminds the woman of her dog.
3. They put things in their bag that need to be done, but never do them, e.g. the piece of paper that the woman wants to get framed.
4. They carry things that may be useful, e.g. the electronic Spanish language interpreter.

## 6 Living in basic conditions

|  | Where did it happen? | What was the problem? | How long did it last? | What did they have to eat/drink? |
|---|---|---|---|---|
| Speaker 1 | climbing a mountain in North Wales | fog – she had to stay on the mountain | one night | a bottle of water and two bananas |
| Speaker 2 | outside Birmingham | traffic jam | about 3 hours | sugared almonds (a kind of sweet) |
| Speaker 3 | an island in the Scilly Isles | fog – he had to stay on the island | one night | Orangina (a kind of orange drink) and some crisps |

## 7 Make it more interesting

*Possible answer:*
I'm afraid my flat is *quite* untidy most of the time. There are piles of *dusty old* newspapers and magazines all over the living room, and *enormous* bookshelves packed with books from floor to ceiling. But at least it's a quiet room and the *antique wooden* table in the middle is *very* elegant.

I *normally* sleep in the bedroom next to the living room, but I have a *tiny* spare bedroom *as well*. It's full of *useless* junk and *pretty* chilly in the winter, but there is an old *electric* fire and a *foldaway* bed which I keep for *unexpected* guests.

The kitchen is *also very* basic with *just* a few *essential* items such as cooker and a fridge. The one nice thing though, is that it is on the tenth floor of a block of flats with *absolutely* fantastic views of the *surrounding* countryside.

## 9 Visual dictionary

1. curtain    2. beach umbrella    3. wellington boots
4. lampshade    5. paint roller    6. sleeping bag
7. tins of paint    8. foldaway bed    9. hi-fi speaker
10. bike    11. trunk    12. picture frame
13. clothes brush    14. barbecue    15. electric fan
16. brush and comb    17. shoehorn    18. bucket
19. spade

# 13 WHO IS REALLY ON TRIAL?

## 1 We wouldn't get wet because …

*Possible answers:*

1. lost; wouldn't matter; you don't need one to go to the island
2. invented; would be; you could see what problems lay ahead
3. didn't have; wouldn't be; you could take more time off in the winter
4. wouldn't matter; barked; you could put cotton wool in your ears
5. would be; died; left; you might feel guilty
6. lost; would be; there is so much unemployment in my profession

## 2 It's the place where you …

*Possible answers:*

1. police station    2. young offender    3. Burglary
4. a place where    5. a person who
6. the thing/money that/which
7. who tells the court what they know about a crime
8. (that) criminals are given for serious crimes    9. the group of people who decide if the defendant is guilty or innocent    10. is the place where trials take place

## 3 The sound of money

### A

2. What is the p<u>u</u>nishment for dr<u>u</u>g trafficking?
3. The p<u>u</u>blic don't tr<u>u</u>st the g<u>o</u>vernment.
4. We m<u>u</u>st reduce <u>u</u>nemployment. (*Must* can be pronounced with /ʌ/ if it is emphatic, but often it is pronounced as /ə/.)
5. It was a t<u>ou</u>gh decision for the j<u>u</u>dge.
6. We need j<u>u</u>stice for every<u>o</u>ne.

## 4 It's similar and different

### A

1. Correct
2. cheese is usually solid
3. whereas murder (kidnapping, assault, etc.) is a crime against people
4. Correct
5. Correct
6. whereas smoking (drinking, taking drugs, etc.) isn't
7. except that blouses are usually worn by women
8. Correct

### B

*Possible answers:*

1. is usually spoken
2. you usually stand up in a shower and sit or lie in a bath
   (*or* a shower is usually quicker than a bath)
3. buses are cheaper (*or* walking is free)
4. marmalade is made of oranges or lemons or grapefruit (is made of citrus fruits)
5. going to the theatre in that it is cheaper
6. Meeting your friends for dinner is relaxing

## 5 Plants and burglars

### C

Police in Essex are *advising* the public and *office* owners to grow certain *types* of prickly *plants* near their property to deter *burglars*. They believe that such plants will make it more *difficult* for intruders to *break into* homes and buildings. People who are interested in finding out more *information* about the scheme can get a *leaflet* from the police station.

## 6 How to beat car theft

1. Every 75 seconds.
2. More than 425,000.
3. 100,000.
4. 1 in 4 (25%).
5. Mark the vehicle identity number in different places in the car.
   Park in well-lit areas and not always in the same place.
   Don't leave car documents in the car.
   Don't leave valuables in the car where they can be seen.
   Get a portable or coded radio.
   Fit a car alarm.

## 7 That's the woman who …

1. That's the place where we got married after the war ended.
2. That's the box I found behind the house.
3. That's the dog that saved the boy who fell in the river.
4. That's the criminal who stole the jewellery that/which was found in the car park.
5. That's the present Molly gave me before I went to Indonesia.
6. That's the town where I met Alan before he was arrested.

# 14 TALL STORIES, SHORT STORIES

## 1 When they had left …

1. got on; realised; had left
2. was; had thrown
3. went / had gone; remembered; hadn't cleaned
4. introduced; was; had met
5. joined; didn't say; became; had been
6. rushed, had gone
7. got; was; hadn't done
8. had never seen; walked; understood; liked

## 2 Excuses, excuses

*Possible answers:*

1. I had to work late last night and I overslept.
2. but I got lost on my way here.
3. I'm really sorry, but I got held up in the traffic.
4. I'm terribly sorry, but my car broke down and I had to wait ages for a mechanic to arrive.
5. I'm really sorry, but I had a puncture on the way here.

### 3 What could it be?

*Possible answers:*
1. a bird     2. an alarm clock
3. a bike, a motor bike, a car, etc.
4. a train, a bus, a coach     5. a horse, a donkey
6. a car     7. a party, a wedding, a reception     8. a story

### 4 Find the right word

1. imaginative     2. suspiciously     3. cancelled
4. death     5. obsessed     6. enjoyable     7. memorise
8. disappeared     9. astonished     10. creative

### 5 I never forget a face (I)

1. False (He can't remember names.)     2. True
3. True     4. True     5. False     6. True

### 6 I never forget a face (II)

1. the narrator     2. the other man     3. the narrator
4. the other man     5. the other man
6. the other man     7. the narrator     8. the narrator
9. the narrator     10. the other man

### 7 Film synopsis

*Possible answer:*
In the film *Tootsie*, Dustin Hoffman played an actor who couldn't find work. Then one day he heard about a female part in a soap opera, so he dressed up as a woman and went for an audition. Incredibly, no one realised he was a man and he got the part. After that, he became very successful and famous, but he never told the rest of the cast that he was a man.

After a while, he fell in love with the leading lady, Jessica Lange, and although they became great friends, he couldn't show his true feelings. Eventually he revealed that he was a man on a live broadcast of the soap. At the end of the film, Jessica Lange fell in love with him.

### 9 Visual dictionary

1. lake     2. cliff     3. wood     4. bench     5. goat
6. path     7. lawn     8. fence     9. bushes     10. gallop
11. dive     12. hop     13. creep     14. throw
15. land     16. skid     17. light

## 15 LOVE THY NEIGHBOUR

### 1 I've been waiting for ages

1. returned     2. been walking     3. lost; seen
4. been writing; finished
5. been waiting (*waited* is possible but less likely)
6. understood     7. *both*     8. been; written
9. been trying (*tried* is possible but less likely)
10. known

### 2 You promised to help

1. d     2. e     3. b     4. f     5. i     6. h     7. a     8. c
9. g

### 3 More acts of kindness

1. A *tramp* is a person who lives on the streets and has no home.
2. A *donation* is a sum of money given to a charity.
3. *Hectic* is busy.
4. *Kids* is an informal word for *children*.
5. A *natter* is an informal word for a *conversation*.
6. If you *cheer somebody up*, you make them feel happier when they have been depressed.
7. If you *give up* your seat, you let somebody else sit in it.
8. *Quarrel* means *argue*.

### 4 Sounds and spelling

1. different     2. different     3. same     4. same
5. different     6. same     7. different     8. different

### 5 A group of wolves

1. Because they don't have destructive human emotions such as greed and envy.
2. It confirms their position in the pack.
3. Because if a single wolf is seriously injured, it is bad for the whole pack.
4. In case anything happens to the natural mother.

### 6 The Living Flag

1. a lot of red, white and blue baseball caps
2. June 1945
3. to stand
4. the national anthem
5. the heat
6. Herman
7. ordered everyone around
8. to see the flag
9. ran up to the roof to see the flag
10. unbelievable
11. went up to the roof
12. hours

### 9 Visual dictionary

1. taking a photograph of someone
2. taking someone's trolley back
3. offering someone a lift
4. planting a tree
5. letting someone go first
6. picking up litter
7. sharing an umbrella with someone
8. giving money to someone
9. offering to carry someone's shopping
10. pushing someone's car

## 16 YES AND NO

### 1 Find the mistakes

1. They didn't see me.
2. I told him not to go.
3. I'm afraid he didn't have a dictionary.
4. Young people don't have to do military service in Britain.

5. A: Is it going to rain tomorrow?
   B: I hope not.
6. They hardly ever go to the cinema.
7. He has never been there.
8. We probably won't see them before next week.
9. I didn't see anything.
10. She heard nothing but I'm sure there was a noise.
11. A: I can't understand this question.
    B: Neither can I.
12. He was dissatisfied with the course.
13. I don't agree with you.
14. I don't think anyone can come.

## 2  I wish I knew ...

**A**

*Possible answers:*
1. I wish I had more money
2. I wish I had my umbrella
3. I wish I could speak French
4. I wish I had straight hair
5. I wish it was Sunday
6. I wish I had some sunblock
7. I wish I could open the window
8. I wish I had more time

## 3  Agreeing with each other

**A**

| | |
|---|---|
| 1. Neither can I. | 5. So have I. |
| 2. Neither do I. | 6. Neither do I. |
| 3. So do I. | 7. Neither did I. |
| 4. Neither have I. | 8. Neither do I. |

**B**

See tapescript on page 135.

## 4  What's the opposite?

**A**

| | |
|---|---|
| careless | dishonest |
| useless | disobedient |
| unsuccessful | dissatisfied |
| painless | disorganised |
| unhelpful | unsatisfactory |
| tactless | unreliable |
| thoughtless | unpleasant |
| harmless | ungrateful |

**B**

*Possible answers:*
1. I was dissatisfied with the results.
2. The weather was terrible so it was very unpleasant.
3. My watch is unreliable, so I need to check it very often.
4. My dog is very disobedient; it does nothing I tell it.
5. She's very dishonest; she never tells the truth (she always tells lies)
6. He's very tactless, so I'm sure he'll say something rude.
7. They were very ungrateful and they all said that my comments were useless and very unhelpful.
8. He's careless and disorganised so I think his work will be unsatisfactory.

## 5  When *yes* means *no*, and *no* means *yes*

| Head actions | Description | Meaning |
|---|---|---|
| 1. The head moves vertically up and down. | The head nod | *Yes* almost everywhere |
| 2. The head moves from side to side. | The head shake | *No*/disagree/ bewildered |
| 3. The head turns sharply to one side and then back to the neutral position. | The head twist | *No* (in parts of Ethiopia) |
| 4. The head moves rhythmically from side to side. | The head sway | *Maybe yes, maybe no* in parts of Europe; *yes* in some other countries |
| 5. The head is tilted sharply back and returns less sharply to the neutral position. | The head toss | *No* in Greece and parts of the Mediterranean |

## 6  Saying *no* politely

See tapescript on page 136.

## 9  Visual dictionary

**A**

| | **B** |
|---|---|
| obedient – disobedient | never |
| everybody – nobody | hardly ever |
| nervous – confident | rarely/seldom |
| grateful – ungrateful | occasionally |
| cruel – kind | quite often |
| innocent – guilty | often |
| admit – deny | always |
| agree – disagree | |

**C**
1. breakfast, lunch    2. starter, main course
3. primary school, secondary school    4. adolescent, adult    5. second, minute    6. year, century
7. middle, end

## 17  PACKAGING

### 1  A packet of biscuits, please

| | | |
|---|---|---|
| 1. can | 5. packets | 9. bag/carrier bag/box |
| 2. tube | 6. bucket | 10. jar |
| 3. bowl | 7. cartons | |
| 4. jug | 8. box | |

### 2  How many, how much, how far

| *horizontal* | *vertical* |
|---|---|
| inch | quarter |
| couple | pint |
| several | kilos |
| pound | dozen |
| litre | pair |
| millimetre | few |
| mile | hundred |
| | loads |
| | weigh |

### 3 Building words and shifting stress

| Noun | Adjective |
|------|-----------|
| power | powerful |
| simplicity | simple |
| danger | dangerous |
| mystery | mysterious |
| elegance | elegant |
| luxury | luxurious |
| glamour | glamorous |
| security | secure |
| history | historical/historic |
| similarity | similar |

### 4 That's not what I asked for

Dear Sir

Holiday no HO56: Receipt no A1032

I am writing to express my dissatisfaction with the accommodation provided for my wife and myself from 11–24 August.

I booked the above holiday at your office on 16 February. At that time, I was promised a room with a private bathroom, air-conditioning, and a balcony; this was confirmed in your letter of 20 February (enclosed). When we arrived, the room given to us had none of these facilities. After we complained, the manager told us your company had made a mistake, and unfortunately no other rooms were available that week.

We were also surprised to find that the price included continental breakfast but not English breakfast, which was extra.

In view of these facts, I think we are entitled to a partial refund of the amount we paid, and I look forward to hearing from you as soon as possible.

Yours faithfully

### 6 Sorry, I got it wrong

See tapescript on page 136, where the changes are underlined.

### 9 Visual dictionary

1. loaf of bread
2. bunch of grapes
3. piece of toast/bread
4. piece of cake
5. lump of sugar
6. spoonful of sugar
7. pinch of salt
8. sheet/piece of paper
9. ball of string
10. pack of cards
11. clove of garlic
12. bunch of flowers
13. bar of soap
14. bar of chocolate

## 18 HONESTLY SPEAKING

### 1 Get it right

1. I told her that I would be late for dinner.
2. Did she tell you she was going to last night's meeting?
3. I didn't ask her what the problem was.
4. He said it was very cold in Moscow at that time of the year.
5. She asked him if he had been there before.
6. The policeman asked me what time I got home.
7. He asked her if she needed any money.
8. She told me to do my homework.
9. We said we had to go out, so we couldn't go to the party.
   (or We said we have to go out, so we can't go to the party.)
10. She was telling me that her brother had a lot of debts.
11. He wanted the hotel to refund his money.
12. I promised to buy the flat.

### 2 How did they say it?

1. He congratulated Marilyn on passing her exam.
2. He offered to do the washing up.
3. He accused her of lying to him.
4. He thanked David for helping him.
5. He threatened to give the job to someone else if she didn't finish by six o'clock.
6. He admitted he broke it (or he had broken it).
7. He refused to look after her dog again.
8. He praised her for saving the child's life.

### 3 Compounds and word partnerships

**A**

| | |
|---|---|
| inflation rate | trade agreement |
| peace talks | political party |
| foreign policy | multi-party election |
| public figure | industrial dispute |
| government minister | newspaper report |

**B**

1. trade(s) union
2. foreign exchange
3. industrial estate
4. Prime Minister
5. exchange rate
6. public relations officer
7. peace-keeping
8. presidential election

### 4 Good news and bad news

1. defeat
2. depressing
3. disaster
4. weaknesses
5. peace/compromise
6. injustice
7. gone wrong
8. admitted
9. failure
10. fall

### 5 Does your job make you lie?

**A**

Karan Lavida and Sandra Grant

**B**

1. No   2. Yes   3. No   4. Yes   5. Yes

### 6 Honestly!

See the tapescript on page 136.

## 7 She said in her letter that ...

Next month we're thinking of coming down to London for a weekend. Paul is attending a one-day conference just outside London, and I'm hoping to get a couple of days off work. Then I can travel down to Kingston with Paul – that's where the conference is – and afterwards we can spend the weekend in London. My brother actually lives very near Kingston, so he has invited us to stay at his place. But we'd really like to take you out for dinner on the Saturday evening if you are both free. That's Saturday the 15th, but I'll give you a ring later in the week to finalise the details. Until then,

Best wishes,

# 19 PLAIN ENGLISH

## 1 Familiar symptoms

1. bite
2. blank
3. shake
4. thread; argument
5. stammer
6. anxiety
7. feel; sweat
8. dry; tense

## 2 Tell them what you think

*Possible answers:*
1. Yes, you ought to go if you want to catch your bus.
2. You'd better take a taxi, then.
3. I think you should consider a different career.
4. Yes, the government ought to build more homes. (*Had better* is not possible in this question.)
5. You should have a word with him in that case.
6. Well, you'd better start cleaning now.
7. Yes, the government should really spend more on education and less on defence. (*Had better* is not possible in this question.)
8. Well, you'd better answer it, then.

## 3 Fear of flying

to overcome; going; taking; to go; finding out; to travel; to live; explaining; to reduce; practising; to get on; using

## 4 Employees and employers

### A

| Noun | Person | Adjective | Verb |
|---|---|---|---|
| employment | employer employee | (un)employed | employ |
| application | applicant | — | apply (for) |
| education | educationalist educator | educational | educate |
| government | governor/MP | governmental | govern |
| consultation | consultant | — | consult |
| interview | interviewer interviewee | — | interview |
| specialisation | specialist | specialised | specialise (in) |

### B
1. applied
2. educational
3. unemployed
4. consultants
5. specialises
6. govern
7. employs
8. interviewer; applicant

## 6 Keep it simple!

### A
1. d  2. b  3. a  4. e  5. f  6. c

### B
*Possible answers:*
Dear Mrs Cathcart,
I'm sorry I couldn't come to the annual policy ...

Dear Mr Crow,
Could I possibly take a week off at the beginning of August? I appreciate this will be very inconvenient, but ...

Dear Jacob,
As I can't get out easily at the moment, I would be very grateful if you could buy the following items of food for me ...

Dear Mr and Mrs Lisard,
I am sorry to say that the bank cannot give you a loan ...

## 7 My mind went completely blank

Speaker 1: 1. She had to read aloud a story she had written.
2. She felt scared and nervous.
3. It was fine because others said they liked her story.

Speaker 2: 1. Walking home in the dark, she thought someone was following her.
2. Her mind went blank, her hands were sweating and her mouth went dry.
3. It was OK – the person behind was just a woman with an umbrella.

Speaker 3: 1. She had to make a speech at a christening.
2. The night before she was OK, but when she stood up she was nervous, shaking and her mind went blank.
3. She forgot the baby's name and thanked everyone for coming to the funeral.

# 20 ART AND SOCIETY

## 1 What's a forgery?

### A
1. f  2. e  3. b  4. h  5. d  6. c  7. a  8. g

### B
*Possible answers:*
1. A self-portrait is a drawing or painting you do of yourself.
2. A gallery is a place where works of art are shown / put on display.
3. A landscape is a drawing or painting of the countryside.
4. To display means to show something so that people can see it, often in a museum.

## 2 A(n), the, or nothing at all

See page 139 in your Class Book.

## 3 We've been sold a forgery

1. A well-known artist illustrated all the books.
2. You should declare foreign currency when you arrive at Customs.
3. All the drawings of the accused have to be done from memory later.
4. Private art collections cannot usually be visited without special arrangements.
5. In Switzerland, bank notes are replaced very regularly, before they begin to look old.
6. People on low incomes shouldn't be charged entrance fees.

## 4 A self portrait that's forgery-proof

**A**
1. water    2. bullet    3. sound    4. shock

**B**
1. defence    2. control    3. service    4. confidence

## 5 Dear Vincent ...

1. van Gogh likes Livens's paintings, ideas and personality.
2. He probably hasn't got much money. He finds Paris more expensive than Antwerp and hasn't much money for models.
3. He is painting flowers.
4. He is optimistic.

| Words to do with painting: | Words to do with finance: |
|---|---|
| art | dear |
| artists | sell |
| master | to lack funds |
| impressionists | a sale |
| pictures | dealer |
| nude figure | price |
| landscape | |
| models | |
| figure painting | |
| harmonise/harmony | |
| an intense colour | |
| to exhibit | |

## 6 I know what I like

| | Tony | Ian | Patience | Julia |
|---|---|---|---|---|
| Picture 1 (the bath) | ✓ | ✓ | ✓ | ✗ |
| Picture 2 (the blue vase) | ✗ | ✓ | ✗ | ✓ |
| Picture 3 (the café) | ✓ | ✗ | ✓ | ✓ |

## 9 Visual dictionary

1. portrait    2. landscape    3. self-portrait    4. artist
5. postcards    6. cartoon    7. statue
8. abstract painting    9. sculpture    10. jug    11. vase
12. jewellery

## 21 DARE YOURSELF TO SUCCEED

### 1 Letter of explanation

Dear Mr Carter,

I am writing this letter because I am too embarrassed to speak to you in person.

When I *applied* for the job as a trainee in the first place, I did not notice the reference to German in the *advertisement*. If I *had noticed* it, I wouldn't *have applied* for the job. However, when you invited me for an *interview* and you asked me if I could speak German, I was very embarrassed and I'm afraid I *lied* to you. In actual fact, I did study German at school, but I was never very good at it.

I know I should *have told* you the truth, but if I *had been* honest, you wouldn't *have given* me the job, and I would *have been* heartbroken. Since joining the company I have *tried* once again to learn German, but I'm afraid it's hopeless.

Now you know the truth you will probably want me to *leave* at once. However, I would like you to know that I have enjoyed working here very much and I have appreciated the help that I have received from all my *colleagues*.

I am very sorry for what I've done.

Yours *sincerely*,

### 2 What follows what?

1. I am not worried about losing my job.
2. She is very satisfied with my work.
3. She wants to build up her reputation.
4. I get on well with my boss.
5. She is very upset that I let her down.
6. I am going on a course in the autumn.
7. She burst into tears when I told her.
8. She is responsible for the project.

### 5 A chance meeting

*Possible answers:*
Robbie would not have become a doctor,
if his father hadn't ignored the car behind him.
if his father hadn't asked Dr Plum for a favour.
if he hadn't sent off his school report.
if Dr Plum hadn't given him a summer job.
if he hadn't enjoyed his work at the hospital.
if Dr Plum hadn't given him a good reference.

### 6 Different lives

Speaker 1 is good at riding. She started when a friend's car broke down and she gave the friend a lift to a riding school. The friend then persuaded her to have a lesson.

Speaker 2 is good at decorating. He started when his decorator broke a leg and couldn't decorate his flat for him. He then decided to do it himself and soon realised he was very good at it and enjoyed it.

## 7 A letter of application

I am replying to the advertisement in *The Times* of 12 May for a company interpreter.

I have a degree in modern languages and diplomas from The Institute of Linguists in Spanish, Italian, German and Polish. I also speak a little Japanese.

I have been working as a translator and interpreter for eight years. My first job was in the Bank of Credit and Commerce where I travelled with managers to conferences and meetings throughout Europe. In 1994 I moved to British Water, and I have been there ever since.

I can/could attend an interview immediately. If my application is/were successful, I will/would need to give my present employer one month's notice.

I look forward to hearing from you.

## 10 Visual dictionary

1. abseiling   2. rock climbing   3. canoeing
4. hiking   5. sailing   6. windsurfing   7. surfing
8. parachuting   9. gliding   10. water skiiing
11. hang gliding   12. cycling   13. camping
14. horseriding   15. birdwatching

## 22 FORCES OF NATURE

### 2 Transformations

1. We can't make a decision unless we have all the facts.
2. I wouldn't open the door unless I knew the person.
3. Unless it stops raining, I won't go out.
4. They will lose the election unless they communicate better with the voters.
5. I won't hire a car unless it's absolutely necessary.
6. I wouldn't work for a living unless I had to.
7. Unless they give us more money, we'll have to close the hospital.
8. She'll get ill unless she eats more.

### 3 Parts of speech

 1. poverty
 2. sickness
 3. powerful
 4. Wisdom
 5. relieve
 6. unsuccessful
 7. survival
 8. healthy
 9. environmental
10. destroyed

## 5 Fight disease through food

| Foods that help you live longer | Reason |
| --- | --- |
| 1. nuts | reduce the risk of heart disease |
| 2. wine (in moderation) | protects the heart |
| 3. garlic | thins the blood – good for the heart |
| 4. onions | kill bacteria, fungi and viruses |
| 5. green tea | reduces certain types of cancer |
| 6. fish | thins the blood, reduces inflammation and may protect against colon cancer |

The text also says that fresh fruit, vegetables and whole grains, are part of a healthy diet.

## 6 I couldn't get used to that

| | problem |
| --- | --- |
| Speaker 1 | driving on the right |
| Speaker 2 | the heat |
| Speaker 3 | foreign coins |

## 9 Visual dictionary

**insects:**   1. bee   2. mosquito   3. spider
4. cockroach   5. wasp   6. fly   7. ant   8. beetle
**reptiles:**   9. snake   10. frog   11. lizard
12. crocodile
**mammals:**   13. mouse   14. rat   15. fox
16. tortoise   17. rabbit   18. squirrel   19. donkey

# IRREGULAR VERBS AND PHONETIC SYMBOLS

## Irregular verbs

| Infinitive | Past simple | Past participle |
|---|---|---|
| be | was/were | been |
| become | became | become |
| begin | began | begun |
| bend | bent | bent |
| bite | bit | bitten |
| blow | blew | blown |
| break | broke | broken |
| bring | brought | brought |
| build | built | built |
| buy | bought | bought |
| can | could | (been able) |
| catch | caught | caught |
| choose | chose | chosen |
| come | came | come |
| cost | cost | cost |
| cut | cut | cut |
| do | did | done |
| draw | drew | drawn |
| dream | dreamt | dreamt |
| drink | drank | drunk |
| drive | drove | driven |
| eat | ate | eaten |
| fall | fell | fallen |
| feel | felt | felt |
| fight | fought | fought |
| find | found | found |
| fly | flew | flown |
| forget | forgot | forgotten |
| get | got | got |
| give | gave | given |
| go | went | gone (been) |
| have | had | had |
| hear | heard | heard |
| hit | hit | hit |
| hold | held | held |
| hurt | hurt | hurt |
| keep | kept | kept |
| know | knew | known |
| learn | learnt | learnt |
| leave | left | left |
| lend | lent | lent |
| let | let | let |
| lie | lay | lain |
| lose | lost | lost |
| make | made | made |
| mean | meant | meant |
| meet | met | met |
| pay | paid | paid |
| put | put | put |
| read /riːd/ | read /red/ | read /red/ |
| ride | rode | ridden |
| ring | rang | rung |
| rise | rose | risen |
| run | ran | run |
| say | said | said |
| see | saw | seen |
| sell | sold | sold |

| Infinitive | Past simple | Past participle |
|---|---|---|
| send | sent | sent |
| set | set | set |
| shake | shook | shaken |
| shine | shone | shone |
| shoot | shot | shot |
| show | showed | shown |
| shut | shut | shut |
| sing | sang | sung |
| sit | sat | sat |
| sleep | slept | slept |
| speak | spoke | spoken |
| spell | spelt | spelt |
| spend | spent | spent |
| stand | stood | stood |
| steal | stole | stolen |
| swim | swam | swum |
| take | took | taken |
| teach | taught | taught |
| tell | told | told |
| think | thought | thought |
| throw | threw | thrown |
| understand | understood | understood |
| wake | woke | woken |
| wear | wore | worn |
| win | won | won |
| write | wrote | written |

## Phonetic symbols

### Vowels

| Symbol | Example |
|---|---|
| /iː/ | see |
| /i/ | happy |
| /ɪ/ | big |
| /e/ | bed |
| /æ/ | sad |
| /ʌ/ | sun |
| /ɑː/ | car |
| /ɒ/ | pot |
| /ɔː/ | taught |
| /ʊ/ | pull |
| /uː/ | boot |
| /ɜː/ | bird |
| /ə/ | among |
|  | produce |
| /eɪ/ | date |
| /aɪ/ | time |
| /ɔɪ/ | boy |
| /əʊ/ | note |
| /aʊ/ | town |
| /ɪə/ | ear |
| /eə/ | there |
| /ʊə/ | tour |

### Consonants

| Symbol | Example |
|---|---|
| /b/ | back |
| /d/ | dog |
| /ð/ | then |
| /dʒ/ | joke |
| /f/ | far |
| /g/ | go |
| /h/ | hot |
| /j/ | young |
| /k/ | key |
| /l/ | learn |
| /m/ | make |
| /n/ | note |
| /ŋ/ | sing |
| /p/ | pan |
| /r/ | ran |
| /s/ | soon |
| /ʃ/ | fish |
| /t/ | top |
| /tʃ/ | chart |
| /θ/ | thin |
| /v/ | view |
| /w/ | went |
| /z/ | zone |
| /ʒ/ | pleasure |

### Stress

Stress is indicated by a small box above the stressed syllable.
Example: advertisement

# ACKNOWLEDGEMENTS

**Authors' acknowledgements**

We would like to thank Stephen Slater for his original inspiration in the development of *True to Life*.

We are also very grateful to Gillian Lazar for her continued support and perceptive criticisms on the final manuscript.

Friends and colleagues have given us permission to use their ideas and activities – or in some cases given us inspiration. We would therefore like to thank Philip Dale, Clare Fletcher, Jackie Gresham, Frances Eales, Susan Barduhn, Terry Miles, Tim Shirra and Frances Gairns. As ever, a big thank you to all our colleagues at International House and The London School of English for their ideas, support and kindness.

We would also like to express our gratitude to writers whose work has influenced us in specific activities: Trisha Hedge, Jill Hadfield and Mark Bartram and Richard Walton.

At Cambridge University Press, we would like to thank James Dingle for his coordination of the pilot edition, and very sincere thanks to Kate Boyce for her excellent management of the project and unfailing support. Helena Gomm's contribution has been immense and we have much appreciated her humour; we are also most grateful to Nick Newton and Randell Harris for their impressive and stylish design and production work.

We would like to thank Martin Williamson for his considerable help and guidance on the listening material and to all the actors involved and to the staff of AVP.

Finally, our thanks go to the commissioning editor, Peter Donovan, who set the project in motion, and to the rest of the staff at Cambridge University Press.

**The authors and publishers would like to thank the following institutions and teachers for their help in testing the material and for the invaluable feedback which they provided:**

AVL, Paris, France; BTL, Paris, France; Diann Gruber, Paris, France; Associazone Culturale Delle Lingue Europee, Bologna, Italy; British Council, Milan, Italy; Civica Scuola di Lingue, Milan, Italy; Cambridge English Studies, La Coruña, Spain; Roger Scott, Bournemouth, UK; Hampstead Garden Suburb Institute, London, UK.

**The authors and publishers are grateful to the following copyright holders for permission to reproduce copyright material. While every endeavour has been made, it has not been possible to identify the sources of all material used and in such cases the publishers would welcome information from copyright sources. Apologies are expressed for any omissions.**

p. 17: *The Times* for the article 'Could this be the girl who will outrun men' by Andrew Alderson – 5/12/92 and artwork by Phil Green; pp. 22–3: *The Independent* for the article 'Magnum force in high heels' by Reggie Nadelson – IND April 1992; p. 27: *Marie Claire* for the extract 'Love-hate relationships' – 11/92; p. 30: Sue Townsend for the extract from *The Secret Diary of Adrian Mole*, published by Methuen, reproduced by permission of Reed International Books; p. 38: *The Independent* for the article 'Back on course' by Jonathan Sale – IND 20/3/94; p. 52: *The Guardian* for the article 'Rude noises on the phone' by Andrew Martin; p. 67: *The Guardian* for the article 'Burglars in for a sharp shock' by Duncan Campbell; p. 78: Garrison Keillor for the extract on cassette from *Lake Wobegon Days*, published and reproduced by permission of Faber and Faber Ltd; p. 86: W. Foulsham for the extract from *Basildon Bond: Letters for Every Occasion*, reproduced by permission of the copyright holders W. Foulsham & Co. Ltd, Slough, England; p. 87: *The Observer* for the article 'Food facts: alimentary forces at work in one world' – 30/1/94; p. 92: *The Independent* for the article 'Does your job involve telling lies' – Opinion column IOS 13/3/94.

**The authors and publishers are grateful to the following illustrators and photographic sources:**

**Illustrators:** David Barnett: p. 106; David Downton: p. 82; Nicky Dupays: pp. 47, 62, 97; Max Ellis: pp. 9, 53, 95; Philip Emms: pp. 36, 60, 87; Martin Fish: pp. 41, 67, 80, 111; Spike Gerrell: p. 35; Sue Hillwood-Harris: pp. 55, 68, 96; Terry Kennett: pp. 30, 75; Joanna Kerr: pp. 11, 56; Amanda MacPhail: pp. 116, 117, 118, 120, 121, 122, 123, 124, 125, 127, 128, 129, 130; Mark Peppé: pp. 72, 78; Giovanna Pierce: p. 13; Tracy Rich: pp. 15, 45, 51, 66, 85, 101.

**Photographic sources**: Ace Photo Agency: pp. 92*tr* (photo Mauritius) and 108 (Mauritius); Allsport UK: p. 6*r* (Duffy); Barnaby's Picture Library: p. 92*bl* and *br* (both Lewis); Bridgeman Art Library: p. 103; Camera Press: p. 92*tl* (Open); Mary Evans Picture Library: p. 28; Ronald Grant Archive: p. 73*l* and *r*; Hearing Dogs for the Deaf: p. 12 (two); Hutchison Library: p. 92*cl* (Highet); The Image Bank: pp. 38 (Hamilton) and 70 (de Lossy); Kobal Collection: p. 73*c* (Columbia); Frank Lane Picture Agency: p. 76 (Newman); National Medical Slidebank: p. 37*t*; Range Pictures: p. 78 (Bettmann Archive); Retna Pictures: p. 37*b* (Acheson); Rex Features: p. 6*l* and *c*.
The photographs on p. 58 were taken by John Birdsall.

*t* = top, *b* = bottom, *c* = centre, *l* = left, *r* = right

Design and DTP by Newton Harris
Picture research by Marilyn Rawlings

**The authors and publishers are grateful to the following for permission to reproduce photographs on the cover:**

Comstock Photo Library, forest; The Image Bank, eyes by David de Lossy, Marc Grimberg, Juan Alvarez and Nancy Brown; Newton Harris, background left; Pictor International, two photos of eyes; Tony Stone Worldwide, island by Pacal Crapet, eyes by Bruce Ayres (two photos), James Darrell and Gerrard Loucel.